THE PHILOSOPHY OF GURU NANAK

A COMPARATIVE STUDY

VOLUME II

By

ISHAR SINGH

Atlantic Publishers & Distributors

B-2, Vishal Enclave, Najafgarh Road

New Delhi - 1 1 0 0 2 7

Published by
Atlantic Publishers & Distributors
B-2, Vishal Enclave, Najafgarh Road,
NEW DFLHI-110027 Ph. : 5413460

1988 EDITION

Price : Vol. I : Rs. 200-00
Vol. II : Rs. 150-00

Printed at :
ANUBHAV ART PSESS
Raghubir Nagar, New Delhi-110027

CONTENTS

PART III

THE GREAT MARCH OF MAN TO TRUTH AND REALITY

FOREWORD

By Dr. (Brig.) S.S. Syalee, M.B.B.S. (Cal.), D.P.M. (Lond.) F.R.C.P. (Edin), F.A.P.A. (U.S.A.)

I have the good fortune of going through the two volumes of the Philosophy of Guru Nanak by Sardar Ishar Singh who has laboured hard for many years to compare the Philosophy of Sikhism with the Philosophy propounded by other great religions of the world and specially that of Hinduism which he has dealt also in a separate volume. This work assumes a special significance in the context of present day world which is torn apart due to discord existing between different religious, social and political faiths and beliefs. Ignorance of the Truth not only widens the gulf between man and man but may foster a spirit of hostility and dissension. Guru Nanak's Philosophy of life brings men and nations closer to each other and helps fostering peace & brotherhood on earth.

"True Teacher is that who brings all men closer to each other" (Guru Nanak, G.G.S., p. 72)

There is an essential unity in all the higher religions and there is no real difference in the ultimate Truths inculcated by various faiths, that there is but one method by which the world has evolved and there is but one goal as admitted by all scriptures. But this basic Truth is one not easily comprehended. The discord existing between different faiths makes it almost impossible to lift the veil and have a look at the grand verity. Guru Nanak's Philosophy removes all doubts and disharmonies and brings the whole humanity on one platform. He teaches us how to control our senses, subdue the evils and passions and teaches the path of 'Sehj' through inhering a loving devotion and meditation on the ONE SUPREME BEING leading to total self-abnegation.

The first Volume of this work has been in print for a number of years and has been well received and acclaimed as a work of great merit and scholarship. The highest achievements of each religion have been fully acknowledged and their contribution to the overall good of the humanity have been affirmed in a manner befitting a true disciple of Guru Nanak who was an embodiment of humility and well wisher of all men inhabiting the earth.

I have no doubt in my mind that these two volumes will not only enlarge the vision of its readers in understanding the subtle differences in different religious philosophies but will bring humanity close to each other by grasping the essential unity of all faiths.

Saket, New Delhi.

Sangat Singh Syalee

MESSAGE

Guru Nanak's Message of Universal Brotherhood,
Love and Peace

I have gone through the manuscript of this book with great pleasure and profit. I find that the author, S. Ishar Singh, has put in very hard labour, in the study of the various religious philosophies dealt with therein and has presented an objective and true picture of these philosophies in this book. It is most desirable that people following different religions should have some knowledge at least about religions other than their own, as that can create better understanding between them. It is evident from the pages of this book that the author, while explaining the different philosophies, has brought out with greater emphasis the common points of different religions. As described by him, Guru Nanak gave all importance to such common points and it is therefore that the spiritual sayings of Hindu Saints, Kabir, Nam Dev, Ravi Das, Sufi Saint Farid and others, find a place in the holy book of the Sikhs, the Adi Granth. The Hindus and Sikhs already have much in common and I have no doubt that in this book a significant attempt has been made to bring the two communities still closer to each other which is the pressing need of the present times. This Message of Guru Nanak can create universal brotherhood love and peace, and should also be transmitted to young boys and girls in all educational institutions. I wish all success to this endeavour of S. Ishar Singh and do hope that this book will attract a large readership as it deserves.

New Delhi

Amba Prasad
M.A., A.M. (U.S.A.), Ph. D.
(Rtd.) Professor of History, Delhi University.

INTRODUCTION

Out of so many religions, which are treated as world religions, four of them originated from the soil of Bharat Desh. Buddhism and Jainism, according to the philosophies recorded in their scriptural books, are atheists not having belief in the existence of any Supreme Power of God. Hinduism, and Sikhism, the other two world religions rising from India, both believe in the existence of God. Guru Nanak is the founder of Sikh religion, which has been further developed and completed by his nine successor Gurus, who also gave it a fundamental book of scripture, the Adi Granth. Hinduism, on the other hand, has neither any single founder nor are its various branches and schools of philosophy based on any single book of scripture. In the first volume of this book the space given to the description of Hinduism is rather limited, with due regard to the requirements of other world religions described therein. However for a deeper understanding of the nature of Hinduism, which is the most ancient theistic religion of the world, it became essential to present to the readers a much more elaborate picture about its various schools of philosophy. Such an understanding became all the more essential in the context of its comparative study with the philosophy of Sikhism. Hinduism and Sikhism are the only indigenous theistic religions of India. They have much in common in the matter of historical background and so far as their social and temporal ties are concerned. But there is also a significant misunderstanding between the two regarding the spiritual side of human life. At present, as against about 2% of Sikhs in India Hindus constitute a majority of about 82% of India's total population. This majority has a capability and a tendency to absorb in itself the new currents of thought arising in this country. Barring a few exceptions the majority of Hindus, have not cared to understand the religion of the Sikhs and consider that all religions arising in India are part of Hinduism. The Sikhs on the other hand, with the knowledge of their own religious principles, are at pains to save themselves from absorption and are clamouring to keep up their separate identity. This situation definitely demands a better understanding between the two, specially at this juncture of India's history. In this second volume of the book, I have therefore made, in my own humble way, a sincere endeavour to present a clear and objective picture of the philosophies of the various schools of Hinduism as well as of the new philosophy of Guru Nanak. This latter philosophy, in fact, has the laudable aim of bringing people of different faiths closer to each other. This is a philosophy of synthesis, which in place of the prevalent ideas of religious superiorities, separateness and divisions, aims at creating conditions of equality, cooperation, love and brotherhood amongst followers of all religions, rather amongst all peoples of our world. As to how such most desirable consequence can be achieved, one of the means on which greatest stress has been laid in this new Philosophy of Guru Nanak, as the readers will find from the pages of this book, is that all human beings may rally and march towards One common all pervading God, who is the source of all Truth, justice, mercy, love and all other qualities of goodness, of which mankind stands in dire need, specially in these present times. Of course, any comments and suggestions from the readers will be welcome.

J-11/76 Rajouri Garden
New Delhi, 21st October 1984.

Ishar Singh

PART I

QUEST FOR TRUTH IN ANCIENT INDIA

1

OUR WORLD

We are a part of a vast and wonderful existence. The vast space with its sun, moon, billions of stars, some of which are much bigger than our sun, and planets around it, inspire a sense of wonder in our hearts. To satisfy that sense of wonder and with the scientific knowledge available in our present age, human beings have been able to walk on the surface of moon and to take photographs of some other planets of our solar system. The American Spaceship Pioneer 11 took six and a half years to reach near the planet Saturn, but this our solar system itself is just a tiny part of the vast universe. The scientists say the nearest star beyond this system is 4.3 light years away, calculated at the speed of 1,86,000 miles per second and it would take our space ship 80,000 years to reach that star, Proxima Centuri. The Milky Way observed by us at night, the scientists hold, contains about 100 billion stars besides about 5000 clouds each about 200 light years in diameter, some having a mass of about one million suns. The Milky Way itself is estimated to be 100,000 light years in diameter, and new stars or suns are being produced from the masses of its clouds.

By experience we are realising that a human being has the power of thinking. This power has, however, a limit and can not go so far as to explain everything we are observing in this universe. Yet by using this power, surmises have been made by scientific brains that this earth of ours had a beginning. It separated from the sun of our solar system some 200 crore years back and after some period it cooled down to become the planet Earth wherein we are living. When and in what form did a human being first appear on this earth is not known but at present we can apply our sense of observation and thinking power on the wonderful machine that the human body is. Such observations reveal that this body is about 60 per cent liquid and the rest 40 per cent solid. The skeleton of 206 bones is bound up with strong strings, the ligaments, so as to make it one whole with movable joints. These bones have a covering of about 660 muscles which are tied with the bones by fibrous bands, the tendons. The skull forms an almost closed box of bones without movable joints as it is to secure the most important organ, the thinking machine or the brain. The heart and lungs, the other two very important organs are also secured by a cage of bones. The muscles have been given the quality of stretching and contracting so as to enable the body to do all sorts of work. Then with a layer of fat over the muscles and to hide its ugliness the whole structure is given a complete covering of skin on which the owner of the body applies soaps and scents to exhibit it as a beautiful thing. To keep this beautiful machine in working order very elaborate arrangements exist for in take of fuel in the form of air and food and their conversion into blood which is pumped out from the heart through blood vessels to all parts of the body. A still more elaborate nervous system spreads out from the brain and spinal cord carrying orders, as if by telephonic wiring to all the voluntary organs hands, feet, eyes etc. to start or stop working, with such method and coordination, that no man made machine can compare to it.

The question arises, is this vast and wonderful universe self made? Is it existing merely by a chance having no other power as its creator and controller? The aggregate human intelligence of the past thousands of years does not subscribe to such an absurd theory. The cosmic entities are all bound by some method and order. This earth of ours and our moon are moving by a method which enables us to calculate precisely the times of the solar and lunar eclipses. The mass of matter is bound up by a method which when discovered by scientists of our time enabled them to break up its tiny component, the atom, and obtain there from a tremendous nuclear power and source of energy. The structure of human body exhibits such a wonderful method that each and every part is performing a specific function giving indication of an intelligent Maker. A human being cannot make its own intelligence, neither can a monkey or other animals make wonderful scientific discoveries as they have not been given intelligence like humans. There are good reasons now to believe that human beings of some other worlds beyond our solar system, possess higher intelligence and technology than available to our scientists. But so many good scientists of our world have not fallen prey to a sense of self pride for their wonderful discoveries and have held that they have simply discovered what is already lying in the bosom of the vast nature and which is made by a higher invisible power of God behind the visible phenomena. For instance the greatest scientist of our modern time, Albert Einstein, says "I believe in God, the God of Spinoza, who reveals Himself in the orderly harmony of universe. I believe that intelligence is manifested through all nature". Numerous other eminent scientists have expressed similar views.

2

THE VEDAS

Their Earlier Concept

Rig Veda has been considered, both by Indian and foreign scholars, as the earliest book of the World which deals with the quest of man in the realm of spirit. Therefore it seems essential for all seekers of Truth and Reality about our world, to understand the main aspects of that original spiritual quest which is represented by the Vedas. As far as may be possible by human endeavours so far made, we should try to understand at what spot on our earth the Vedas first appeared, what was the period of their formation, what writings constitute the Vedic literature and what is the nature of those writings. Undoubtedly this is a vast subject not within easy reach of even the greatest Vedic scholars. Here however a modest attempt is made to understand the matter of fact details about those matters depending, as far as possible, on the writings of eminent Sanskrit and Vedic scholars of India.

More than 2500 years before the commencement of Christian era, human civilisation was flourishing only at a few spots on our earth. Three most prominent spots of this nature were the Nile valley of Egypt, the Euphratus valley of Mesopotamia and the Indus valley of India. The Indus valley civilisation which is also called Harappan civilisation, even though discovered somewhat later than the other two, came to develop, in due course, as the most advanced so far as the human quest in the realm of spirit is concerned. In those early times human population was much thinner than in the modern times, but agricultural and other resources for human sustenance were also undeveloped. Except at the few civilised spots, where people led peaceful settled lives, at many other places groups of people were moving about in search of better living conditions. According to historical, geological and linguistic researches made by eminent investigators, one such group of people entered north-western plain of India in about the year 1500 B.C. and they were called Aryans. This north-Indian plain forms a connecting link of the great Indian peninsula of the south, with the great Himalyan mountain ranges of the north. "And yet it is this plain, which became habitable for man only from ten to five thousand years before our time, that is the cradle of Indian Civilisation" says Prof: Jay Chandra Narang.[1] Regarding the question who were these people who came to be called Aryans and where from they came, the researches made on the same geological and linquistic basis prove that the place of origin of these people was southern part of Europe and Russia. "Thus the linguistic evidence, so far available, leads us to the conclusion that South Russia was the home land of the Aryans"[2] says Dr. B.K. Ghosh. Moving down from the Ural-Altai region of South Russia the Aryans advanced towards south east. The peaceful tribes amongst them settled down in Iran and at some other places from where they passed, while the more adventurous proceeded further towards India. When they arrived in the north-western plain of India they were greatly impressed by its beauty, screne rivers, congenial climate, fertile land and peaceful Himalayan forests. These were in great contrast to dry mountaineous land scape of Iran. Hence they settled down here making this north-western plain of India as their permanent home. Here, of course, to the people of Harappan civilisation, the Aryans were unwelcome intruders and great antagonism and warlike conditions continued between the two peoples for quite some time. The inflow

1. Narang, Jai Chandra, "Regional Structure of India in Relation to Language and History", *Cultural Heritage of India*, Vol. I, 1958, p. 33.
2. Ghosh, Dr. B.K., "The Origin of the Indo-Aryans", *Cultural Heritage of India*, Vol. I, 1958, p. 143.

of the Aryans, which commenced in 1500 B.C., continued for two or three following centuries. Even though they carried some attributes and beliefs of the land of their origin, it is but natural that a people coming to a new land and living there generation after generation, become inhabitants and acquire attributes more of their new country than of the old. Inevitably the Aryan and Harappan cultures got mixed up, to some extent at least, and the former did acquire some influence of the higher civilisation of the latter, even when the Aryans became dominant over the Harappans. The Aryans felt a new heaven opened to them in India and with happier living conditions here they became, in due course, worthy sons of the Indian soil itself. Their minds began to soar high in the realm of spirit and they began to see with awe and wonder the working of cosmic entities. Praise and worship of natural objects like Fire, Sun, Earth and Sky, they carried from their land of origin as such worship was common with all Aryans. Here in their new abode, with green meadows around and snow clad Himalayan mountains within their sight, they delved deep in the mysteries of nature and sublimated the worship of such natural entities to great spiritual heights, and began to compose verses with a feeling of deep gratitude for the benefits they were drawing from them. They attached sublime reverence to each such object of nature, individualised and deified them as their benefactors and began to ask all types of boons from them like gold, cattle, sons, grandsons etc. for a happy life in this world. They composed verses in praise of Agni (Fire), Surya or Savitr (Sun), Prithvi (Earth), Dyu (Sky), Mitra (god of day), Varuna (god of night) and many other natural objects. Formation of water by bursting of clouds into rain impressed them as a most beneficial natural phenomenon and they individualised the rain-god as Indra. As Indra appeared to them striking and piercing the dark clouds, which they called 'Vritra' and this victory of Indra over demon Vritra caused the bursting of rain, Indra became a god of war and victory to the Aryans. The highest number of verses they composed in praise of Indra. Next of Indra the highest number is in praise of Agni. All these verses were-treated as sacred Mantras which the Aryans remembered by heart and passed on to their descendants by oral transmission from generation to generation. Subsequently these Mantras formed part of the foremost scriptural book of the world, the Rig Veda.

Dr. S. Radhakrishnan says "Veda is not a literary work like Bhagvat Geeta or a collection of a number of books compiled at some particular time as the Tripitka of the Buddhists or the Bible of the Christians, but a whole literature which arose in the course of centuries and was handed down from generation to generation through oral transmission. When no books were available memory was strong and tradition exact."[1]

Even though the number of Mantras in praise of Indra embodied in Rig Veda exceeds those in praise of Agni, yet the latter occupied a special position in the minds of Aryan seers or 'Rishis' because it constituted a medium or priest through whom oblations were offered to all other gods in the process of worship by 'Homa'. Swami Sharvananda writes "Agni is also one of the universally acknowledged pre-vedic gods whose worship was prevalent among all branches of the Aryan race. To the primitives fire was the most useful yet the rarest phenomenon of nature and that naturally evoked in the simple minds of the early Aryans a feeling of deep reverence. The very first hymn of the Rig Veda opens with the utterence "Praise be to Lord Agni, the chosen priest the shining one, minister of sacrifice and inviter of gods, possessor of great wealth (R.V.I-1-1)."[2]

The observation of the Nature further led the Aryans to conclude that the universe has three main parts, the sky, the middle space and the Earth. They called them Dyu loka (celestial region), the Antariksa loka (intermediary region), and Bhur loka (terristrial region) and also treated the three gods, Surya or Savitr, Indra, and Agni as the three presiding powers of these regions respectively. These three gods were further multiplied into thirty three, eleven being associated with each region and these were named as twelve Adityas, Eleven Rudras, eight Vasus, Sky and Earth. The process of increasing the

1. Radhakrishnan, Dr. S., "Relation to the Vedas", *The Principal Upanisads*, p. 29.
2. Sharvananda, Swami, "The Vedas and their Religious Teachings", *Cultural Heritage of India*, Vol. I, 1958, p. 192.

number of Aryan gods proceeded still further and about this further augmentation Swami Sharvananda says "These thirty three gods were augmented again into three thousand, three hundred and thirty nine gods as we read in Rig Veda (III-9-9). The great Sayana while commenting on this passage tells us that the original gods are only three and these three thousand three hundred and thirty nine gods are but enumeration of the glories of the thirty three gods referred to above."[1] Sayanacarya, who is mentioned above, lived in 14th century A.D. His commentary on Vedas as well as the Nirukta of Yaska, who lived much earlier, are two sources of utmost importance for interpretation of Vedic Mantras and no modern scholar can do without taking help from these two sources. The scholars who are quoted here do recognise the great value of these two sources, as is evident from their writings.

While observing the three regions of the universe, indicated above, the Aryan minds rose still higher in the realm of wonderful Nature and they realised that the scene of the universe before them was infinite beyond the reach of observation by their eyes. They called this personified Infiniteness as goddess 'Aditi' and she is treated as a single immanent power behind all other gods or as 'Mother of all gods'. The Celestial gods such as Savitr (Sun) are treated as sons of Aditi and are called Adityas.

The Aryan sages were seekers of Truth and Reality and after passing many centuries here in the Indian plain, they were no longer foreigners but became genuine 'Men of India'. When their inquisitive minds pierced deeper and deeper, the realisation dawned to some of them, who were more advanced than others, about the existence of One Supreme Power behind all the numerous deities they had been worshipping. They reconciled their earlier beliefs of worship of many with worship of One Supreme God as the base and ground of the numerous different deities. But that did not mean discarding by them the worship of many which continued unabated as they felt nothing wrong in veneration and worship of all those numerous natural entities whom they had earlier deified. Dr. S. Radhakrishnan

1. *Ibid.*, p. 188.

says' "The Vedic seers were not conscious of any iconoclastic mission. They did not feel called upon to denounce the worship of various deities as disastrous error or mortal sin. They led the worshippers of the many deities to the worship of the One and the Only God by a process of reinterpretation and reconciliation."[1]

The Vedas which contain some verses such as 'Ekam Sat Vipra Bahuda Vedanti' therefore contain the idea of One Supreme God rather in a seed form which sprouted, bloomed and flourished subsequently in the Upanisadic period.

1. Radhakrishnan, Dr. S., "Relation to the Vedas", *The Principal Upanisads*, pp. 40-41.

3

THE VEDAS

Period, Authorship and Nature

From fifteenth to eleventh centuries B.C. is considered as the period of formation of the Vedic Samhitas, as they exist now. It is quite possible that during this period of so many centuries all those sacred Mantras uttered by numerous sages, and which were of high spiritual value, could not be collected in those Samhitas, which literally mean 'Collections' and many might have been left out therefrom. On the other hand it is also possible that some Mantras which were not of adequate spiritual value could have found a place therein as interpolations. Dr. S. Radhakrishnan says, "A good deal of time should have elapsed for this long development (of Vedas). The most of Rig Veda must also have taken time to produce, especially when we remember that what has survived is probably a small part compared to what has been lost".[1] The language of the Vedic Mantras is Sanskrit as it was spoken by the Indian Aryanas of that time and it has some peculiarities which distinguishes it from classical Sanskrit as it developed later on. The Aryans who settled in Iran and those who settled in India, had so many words which exhibited similarity and a common source of their languages. It is believed that the name of the country of Iran is derived from 'Aryanam' meaning 'land of Aryas' because of the settlement of Aryas there. The 'Avesta' the scriptural book of

1. Radhakrishnan, Dr. S., "Relation to the Vedas", *The Principal Upanisads*, p. 27.

Zorastrians of Iran and the Rig Veda of India have therefore many common features. If Rig Veda gods were Varuna and Mitra, the Avestan gods were Ahura and Mithra. Ahura developed to Ahura Mazda as Supreme God of Iranian Zorastrians. If a vedic god of death was Yama an Avestan god was called Yimi and there are other similar signs of a common source of the Rig Vedic and the Avestan languages. Evidence about such a common source of Vedic language is also available from several similar words which were current among Mitanian people of Mesopotamia at the time when Aryans moved out from there towards India.

No doubt a strong belief is current in a section of Hindus of India that Sanskrit language of the Vedas is of divine origin and so are the Mantras of Vedas which according to them were created, in the distant past, at the time of creation of this World by God himself or by Brahma, His Power of Creation. Accordingly about authorship of Vedas on one side there is such a strong belief, and on the other side exists a comprehensive evidence based on research made by scholars of history, philosophy, sciences of Philology (language) and Etymology (words), for instance Suniti Kumar Chatterje, the famous linguistic scholar jointly with three other eminent scholars N.K. Dutt, A.D. Pusalkar and N.K. Bose, says, in the preface to *Cultural Heritage of India*—Vol. I "We have to bid goodby to theories of hoary antiquity for Indian Aryan Culture, which we in India generally look upon as axiomatic. As it has been discussed in some of the papers in this volume, we might look upon the tenth century B.C., the last phase of the Vedic age, as the time when the 'Indian man' came into being. The beginning of the Vedic period may go back to the 14th or 15th century B.C., and outside India, in Iran and in Northern Mesopotamia, to a time when the pre-Vedic Aryans or Indo-Iranian language was current. From the Mitanian and other documents, we have glimpses of the pre-Vedic and pre-Avestan language as it was in use round about 1500 B.C.". They further add "During the centuries that elapsed between the composition of the Mantras which constitute the beginnings of what later came to be called the Rig Veda, and in their incorporation in the Samhita text or codification, the Mantras were handed down in different families and employed at ceremonies so that they were exposed to considerable change. The present text which is preserved through oral transmission represents a fairly late stage in the development of Rig Veda, the language is not homogenious, several divergent forms, some archaic and some representing the language of the time, have crept in."[1]

The Aryans in their land of origin were not a civilised people. They were not having regular houses but were living in huts and could move about freely. After passing several centuries in India the Aryan man was indeed transformed into a 'New Indian Man' who rose high in spirit and his objective was to know the reality about the world they lived in. They saw the reality as far as they could and spoke out their minds. But man is a created being and has limited powers. He cannot catch the Reality with one jump. It is also a natural phenomenon that capacities of human beings differ. Some reach a higher stage in achieving knowledge of Reality than others. This was true of Vedic sages also. Some realised divinity in different natural entities and later on some realised One divine power behind all.

There were seekers of Truth and Reality amongst the Semitic peoples as well. In the year 760 B.C. a Hebrew Prophet Amos declared that God appearing to him said "for three transgressions of Damascus and for four I will not turn away the punishment thereof" (*Holy Bible*—Amos 1-3), and Jews of Israel were surprised and delighted to know that their god had also jurisdiction over their enemy, the people of Damascus. Later on in about the year 540 B.C., the further Reality about One God dawned on the people of Israel when their Prophet second Isaiah made the declaration from God "I am the Lord and there is none else; There is no God besides me" (*Holy Bible*—Isaiah 45-5).

It is no wonder, therefore, if the Vedic sages also came to realise, at some stage the existence of One Supreme God behind all the different deities they had been worshipping earlier.

1. Chatterji, Dr. S.K., Pusalker, Dr. M.A., Dutt, Dr. N., "Editors' Preface", *Cultural Heritage of India*, Vol. I, 1958, p. xlix.

Even then such a stage came to Vedic sages much earlier than the Hebrew Prophets or to any other peoples of the world and it is therefore that Rig Veda is the earliest scriptural book of the world exhibiting human quest in the mysteries of Spirit. Human quest for Reality has always been going on and will go on forever in future because no living being can ever claim that he has discovered the final Reality about God and His Creation. Even though all human beings and all religions have a right to have their own beliefs and a section of Hindus do have a strong belief about the hoary antiquity of the Vedas and their divine origin, another section of them do give credence to the scientific researches made by historians, geologists and Linguistic experts, specially those experts professing Hindu religion, whom we have quoted here. Another such scholar, Dr. C. K. Raja says about authorship of Vedas "The Rig Veda Samhita has nearly 10500 verses grouped into 1017 hymns collected into ten Mandalas (books) of unequal length. These hymns are composed by various poets (or rishis). The first and tenth Mandalas are by many authors of different families, the unity between them is that each of them contains exactly 191 hymns. They are thus placed in the beginning and in the end. The Mandalas from II to VII have complete unity of authorship, II to VI being composed by Grtsamada, Visvamitra, Vamadeva, Atri, Bharadvaja and the poets of their families respectively, while the entire seventh Mandala is by Vasistha. Kanva and his family form the predominant group of authors of the eighth Mandala. The whole of 9th is made up of hymns address to Soma Pavamana; its poets belong to different families. The general arrangement thus places the family hymns, in the middle, the Soma Pavamana Mandala coming immediately afterwords... The internal arrangement within a Mandala places the father's hymns first; the son's hymns follow. But in the fifth Mandala, Suktas 52 and the following composed by Sayavasva precede the Suktas 63 and 64 composed by his father Arcananas. Here the order is reversed because the son had composed far more hymns than the father. Except in the 8th Mandala and in the 9th, which is wholly devoted to Soma Pavamana, everywhere hymns to Agni come first, then those to Indra, followed by those addressed to other deities."[1]

Out of the vast Vedic literature comprising the Samhitas, Brahmanas, Aranyakas and Upanisadas, there is no uniformity of opinion as to what part thereof can be called Sruti or 'Word of God'. The Aranyakas are considered a part of Brahmanas and out of about two hundred Upanisads only sixteen were treated as genuine and authoritative by the Ad Sankracharya. A tradition based on Muktika Upanisads mentions the number of Upanisads as one hundred and eight. A section of Hindus treat all these three parts, the Samhitas, the Brahmanas and the genuine Upanisads, as Sruti and in this section are included also the great Vedic Philosophers such as Sankracharya, Badarayana, the author of Brahma Sutras, and also Sayana who mentions all the three in a common category, in his commentary. Another section and rather a large one, treats the Samhitas and Brahmanas only as the Sruti and yet another says only the four Samhitas, Rig Veda, Yajur Veda, Saman Veda and Atharav Veda are the 'Words of God' and all other are works by human beings. The Yajur Veda Samhita has two parts, the Taittiriya Samhita or Black Yajur Veda and Vajasaneyi Samhita or White Yajur Veda. Several Upanisads are included in and form part of some Samhitas and Brahmanas. For instance Isa Upanisad is part of Vajasaneyi Samhita, Brahadaranyaka Upanisad is part of Satpatha Brahmana, Chandogya forms last eight chapters of Mantra Brahmana and Kena Upanisad is part of Talavakara Brahmana. All the sixteen authentic upanisad are associated with one or the other of the four Vedas. Thus Kausitaki and Aitareya are associated with Rigveda, Isa, Brahadaranyaka and Jabala to White Yajur Veda, Katha, Taittiriya, Kaivalya, Svetasvatara and Narayana to Black Yajur Veda, Kena and Chandogya to Sama Veda and Prasna, Mundaka, Mandukya, and Nrsimhatapani to the Atharva Veda.

The Brahmanas are essentially the interpretation of Mantras

1. Raja, Dr. C.K., "Vedic Culture", *Cultural Heritage of India*, Vol. I, 1958, pp. 199-200.

contained in the Samhitas for the purpose of their application in the performance of Vedic rituals and sacrifices. As we have observed earlier, even though a number of the Mantras of Rig Veda are in worship of Natural objects as minor deities, there are also therein Mantras for the purpose of application in rituals. Dr. V. M. Apte therefore says "The compilation of the Rig Veda Samhita is not governed by the rigid principle of conformity to the order of the sacrificial ritual and though the cults of the fire and the Soma dominate the religion of the Rig Veda even in the early stages, an exclusively ritual character in not to be ascribed to it. While a great number of its hymns were from the first intended to be nothing but sacrificial chants and litanies, and acertain number is connected with magic, a large number of hymns arose independently of the sacrificial rituals though they were actually used later in sacrificial contexts. Certain verses and hymns in the Rig Veda were definitely intended for liturgical employment from the beginning".[1] The three other Vedas contain in some form much that is already contained in the Rig Veda but the Yajur and Saman are predominantly liturgical while Atharva contains much which is being considered as superstition, magic, witch craft with prayers for overcoming adversaries etc. For instance Atharva Veda Mantra III—18 containing a prayer to a plant reads.

> "O Thou of out streched leaves, fortunate god—quickened; powerful, do thou thrust away my rival, make my husband wholly mine."

Another Atharva Veda Mantra VII—50 (52) — 1 reads

> "As the thunderbolt always strikes the tree irresitably, so may I today smite (badh, vidh) the gamblers with the dice."

Whereas in the four Samhitas, there are generally simple prayers to objects of Nature, which excited wonder and veneration in the simple minds of Vedic sages and prompted them to crave from them whatever they needed for their lives, the

1. Apte, Dr. V.M., "Vedic Rituals", *Cultural Heritage of India*, Vol. I, 1958, p. 234-35.

transition from Samhita to the second stage of Brahmanas appears to have been prompted by the inspiration they received from the Rig Veda Sukta No. X-90, the well-known Pursha Sukta. As in this Sukta the Param Pursha or the Supreme Being is indicated to have offered his own sacrifice to create the universe, the Vedic sages felt it was not right for them to go on asking all kinds of boons but offer nothing in return. They, therefore, held that the practical way of worship was offering sacrifices through the processes which came to be recorded in the Brahmanas. It is also evident that the Law of Karma and that of Transmigration of Soul gets original indications in the Brahmanas, as there is hardly any specific mention of these principles in the Samhitas. In the Brahmanas the rewards of sacrifices are mentioned. The offerings made in sacrifices included besides clarified butter, barley bread (purodas). Soma drink, goat, sheep, ox, and rarely horse and still more rarely human. It is considered that Pursha Sukta was chanted at the time of human sacrifice though such a sacrifice might have remained only a theory and hardly a practical one.

Here it may be added that a section of Hindus do not give credence to such sacrifices of living beings. They interpret 'Asvamedha' as not indicating horse sacrifice. In fact they interpret the names of the numerous deities mentioned in the Mantras, contained in the Samhitas, as indicative of One God; relying upon the Sanskrit roots, on which these names are based. For instance 'Agni' is taken as derived from the root 'anchu' meaning 'gatti', 'moving or going' or 'knowing' and hence connoting 'One God' who is 'all knowing'. Of course Sanskrit words admit of different interpretations and it would have been a progressive step for Hindu Religion if the great bulk of Vedic writings contained in the Samhitas and the Brahmanas could have given the impression of worship of One God. But what is evident factually is that a very large section of Hindus, give credence to the worship of numerous minor gods who are worshipped in their temples as images and idols and also the ritualistic worship through sacrifices in Agni and otherwise is still being carried on. Rather there is additions of some further minor gods for the purpose of worship in Hindu Temples. In the Samhitas there is no mention of the trinity of Barhama, Vishnu and Shiva which were subsequently treated as gods of Creation, Sustenance and Dissolution of the world. Of course, Vishnu is mentioned as an aspect of the Surya (Sun) and is one among other aspects such as Mitra, Varuna, Bhaga, Savitr etc. Neither is there in the Samhitas any mention of Rama and Krishna who are being worshipped as incarnations of God.

It appears in the earlier Samhita period of the Vedas, the caste distinctions were not rigid, even though the society was divided in four classes on the basis of the type of work the people were capable of doing. Such class distinctions were not new for Indian Aryans as in Iran and European countries inhabited by other Aryans, such distinctions were also in vogue. In that earlier time it was possible that if someone acquired the capability of a higher class he could change over to that higher class. The instances of this nature are cited about Grtsamada and Visvamitra who were Kashtrias but became Brahmans on account of their work of the spiritual nature. From the later Samhita time and thereafter the Caste system went on acquiring more and more rigidity. The Rig Veda Mantra X-90, the famous Pursha Sukta, is a later time Mantra and its clauses nos. 11 and 12 read.

11. "When they divided Purusa how many portions did they make? What do they call his mouth, his arms? What do they call his thighs and feet?

12. "The Brahman was his mouth, of both his arms was the Rajanya made. His thighs became the Vaisya, from his feet the Sudra was produced".[1]

The Head of human body containing the thinking organ of brain is the highest part which controls the functioning of all parts while feet are the lowest part which do the physical work in obedience to orders from brain. The Pursha Sukta accordingly formed the original basis of the Varna distinctions which subsequently developed to a stage of such great rigidity. The Atharva Veda Mantra V-17-8, similarly has been taken as original Vedic authority for higher privileges of higher castes.

1. Griffith, R.T.H., *Hymns of Rig Veda*, p. 603.

Clause 8 of that Mantra reads.

> "And if (there were) ten former husbands of a woman, not Brahmans—provided a Brahman seized her hand, he is alone her husband".[1]

In the Brahmana period and thereafter Brahmans functioned as a privileged class and sudras were treated not only as the lowest caste but were denied the right of reading or hearing the Vedas.

The Aranyakas, the third part of the Vedas went a step further on the road to Truth. While in Brahmanas the entire stress was on the physical performance of sacrifices, rites and rituals, in the Aranyakas a tendency of speculative worship developed. In fact the Aranyakas were formulated to meet the needs of elderly sages who retired from active life to the serene and peaceful conditions of forests. In those conditions it was difficult also to procure all the elaborate accessories required for Brahmana sacrifices. Those sages therefore began to indulge in deep thinking or meditation. They could not, of course, set aside altogether the rituelistic worship of the Brahmanas, but instead of the physical objects of ritualistic worship they began to adopt symbols in their meditation. They realised that 'prana' or the Vital breath is of the highest importance to man and they began to meditate on prana. Similarly they realised the 'Akasa' or the element of vast space as the omnipresent and eternal object and they began to meditate on it. Also they felt 'Aditiya' the sun and 'Manas' the mind as performing a higher and wonderful part in human existence and they made these, objects of their meditation. This tendency of contemplation and meditation, gradually replaced their ritualistic physical worship by mental research into the Supreme Reality. This brought them nearer to realisation of Brahman. However, such research matured in last and most important part of the Vedas, the Upanisads.

At the point of its journey to the realm of Truth, the world reached its biggest station and that was the Upanisads. The light of realisation dawned on the pure and receptive minds of

1. Mitra, Dr. P., *Life and Society in Vedic Age.*

Vedic sages that One Supreme Conscious Power of Brahman existed behind all the cosmic bodies that they had earlier been praising and worshipping. The greatest discovery of all times was made by those sages that there were no corporeal personalities behind various cosmic entities deserving their praise and worship but there was a single incorporeal Supreme Power of Brahman which deserved to be understood and worshipped. The Brahman was not only, all-pervading Supreme Consciousness or 'Chit' but also all-Truth, 'Sat' and all-Bliss, 'Anand'. If such 'Sat-Chit-Anand' Brahman could be understood and realised in human minds, those minds could also be full of all Truth and all happiness with no vestige of any falsehood and sorrow. This discovery was greatest indeed as it had all the potential of eradicating falsehood and suffering from human beings and creating instead righteousness and happiness. The Vedic sages stressed therefore that realisation, understanding or having knowledge of such Brahman was all important, not the performance of Vedic rituals. In other words the earlier 'Karam Marg' was replaced by 'Gyan-Marg' or the way of Knowledge, in the Upanisadic part of Vedas. These upanisadic sages by unfolding the original knowledge about Brahman, thus left a great heritage for the benefit of the world to come after them, but they wanted further to find out how and where those minds could have a contact with such blissful all-pervading consciousness of Brahman. And they discovered another great Truth that the consciousness inside every human being, was a part of Supreme Consciousness of Brahman and this inner consciousness of man was the nearest and most handy spot to contact with the all-pervading Brahman. Brahman was not separate from the self of man and he was not sitting somewhere apart. Rather the power and capability of human mind, eyes, ears etc. to think, see, hear etc., is, in fact, indicative of the power of Brahman Himself. Just as the working force of wonderful cosmic entities, Sun, Agni, Vayu, Rain etc. is in reality of Brahman Himself, similarly the working force of the various organs of the most wonderful machine, the human body, is also of the Brahman Himself. In both cases nothing can be more senseless, than to say that all these are functioning automatically without any intelligent Power behind them. The

Upanisadic sages, however, say that man could realise the Power of Brahman working in his sense organs if he breaks with or renunciates the outer world and diverts his sense organs from outside to his innerself. The Upanisad declares, "Since He (Brahman) is the Ear of the ear, the Mind of the mind, the Speech of speech, the Life of life, and the Eye of the eye, therefore, the intelligent man, after giving up (self-identification with the senses) and renouncing this world, become immortal"[1]—(Kena Upanisad 1-2). The upanisads are emphatic in declaring that realisation of self is all important and that can bring end of all doubts and sorrows "When to the man of realisation all beings become the very self, then what delusion and what sorrow can there be for that seer of Oneness".[2] —(Isa Upanisad-7). The declarations such as 'Aham Braham asmi' and 'Tat tvam asi' are similarly emphatic declarations to indicate that the self of man is not different from Brahman, Himself. All such utterances are however, flights of sublime emotions and songs of buoyant spirits.

Numerous are Upanisadic Seers and numerous are the Upanisads. Naturally the Upanisads do not construct any specific philosophy which may give a rational and coherent picture of life and the universe. If self is Brahman Himself who suffers death, who transmigrates, who gets rewards of good or bad Karmas, and similar other questions crop up which require a philosophical research also of Truth and Reality. Such philosophical research was attempted in the period subsequent to Upanisadic period and six Darsanas came into existence, which we will discuss briefly in the chapters that follow.

1. Gambhirananda, Swami, (tr. by), *Eight Upanisads*, Vol. I, 1977, p. 40.
2. *Ibid.*, p. 13.

4

THE SANKHYA PHILOSOPHY

No one could have understood what day is had there been no night. The value of light is understood after having experience of darkness. On the one hand if the Upanisadic sages could realise in their minds, the effulgent kindly light of Brahman, on the other hand there were human minds, in that very period of Vedas and Upanisads, who held that Reality was confined only to what they were observing with their main sense organs. Perception only constituted their main instrument of finding out Reality and Truth. Inference (Anumana) had no place and if they observed amoke with their eyes they were not prepared to draw the inference that fire was also existing. Loukya Brahaspati was the originator of such materialistic philosophy in India. Several Vedic Mantras are ascribed to him and these express ideas of being good by human free thinking not by authority of any spiritual power or any Vedic injunctions. Brahaspati's philosophy came to be called, in due course, as Lokayata and it holds that human body is composed of four elements, earth, air, fire and water. The fifth Akasa or ether, not being within human perception, was rejected. Consciousness in human beings is the result of an arrangement of the four elements in a peculiar way as they are in the body, and there is no permanent soul. Nothing survives on death of body and therefore there is no transmigration of soul, neither is there any law of Karma by which rewards accrue for good or bad actions of human beings. Although Brahaspati himself preached goodness by free thinking his followers fell in evil ways. Subsequently they came to be called Charvakyas or people who spoke attractive words, but their philosophy of free thinking and free action led them to evil ways, which invoked vigorous opposition from the believers in Upanisadic philosophy. Ultimately they could not survive in India and were extinct as a class.

However it was on account of the influence of Brahaspati's philosophy which created a materialistic atmosphere opposite to Vedic spirituality and ritualism that gave birth to Buddhism and Jainism in India. While the Upanisadic Philosophy was 'Atmavada' 'which held that Brahman, which was not different from self of man, was the permanent unchanging Reality, the Buddhist philosophy was 'Anatmavada' which held that every thing was in a state of flux and change and there was no permanent unchanging soul or Brahman. While according to Upanisadic philosophy non-realisation of the permanent Reality, of Brahman is due to 'Avidya' or ignorance of man, in accordance with Buddhist philosophy, the professed realisation of anything as permanent Reality is due to 'Avidya' or ignorance of man. Jainism adopted a middle philosophy that soul of man was a permanent reality, but not any Supreme Soul or Brahman. Thus uncounted souls with their differences of forms and merits, became permanent Realities and with such splitting up of One Reality propounded by the Upanisads, the Jaina philosophy was neither 'Atmavada' nor 'Anatmavada' and it was called 'Syadavada'. Such a Jaina philosophy could not have much appeal with the Indian minds which were in search of Reality and hence it has remained stationary during all this long period of more than twenty five centuries. The struggles between Upanisadic and Buddhist philosophies was on a larger scale and a long time affair, firstly because Gautam Buddha had evolved an attractive ethical code free from ritualism and Varna inequalities of the Vedas, and secondly because Buddha himself possessed such a unique personality that he is described as "most Godless but most godlike" man. On the basis of philosophy proper Buddhism further got sub-divided in sub-streams of Vaibhasika, Sautantrika, Vijnana Veda and Madhyamika, but all these sub-systems had the same core that there is no permanent soul or supreme soul of

Brahman. The Indian mind, on the criterion of Reality and Truth, could not, in the long run, acquiese in such Buddhist Philosophy also and Buddhism was almost completely ousted from Indian soil, even though it is existing as a spill over from India, in its adjoining countries. Here in India the quest for Reality and Truth continued unabated and formation of the six Darsanas or schools of philosophy commenced alongwith or even before the rise of Buddhism and Jainism. Whereas Buddhism, Jainism, and also the earlier Lokayata are considered as Heretic or atheistic systems, the six Darsanas are treated as 'Theistic orthodox systems' of Indian philosophy. Their growth proceeded with the background of both the streams of thought that of Atmavada of Upanisads and that of Anatmavada represented mainly by Buddhism. However, all the six Darsanas attempt to base their systems on some authority of the Upanisadic literature. These systems are neither the works of any single author nor they pertain to any single period. The ideas began with some one much earlier and these went on maturing for long periods. The authorship of Sankhya philosophy is ascribed to Kapila. There are good reasons to believe that ideas about Sankhya system existed before the advent of Buddha. It appears therefore, that Kapila lived before Buddha and was the originator of the Sankhya ideas. The Sankhya Parvachna Sutra and the Tatvasamasa whose authorship is generally ascribed to Kapila, were works of a later period completed by Kapila's successors, like Asuri, Panchasikha, Gargya and Uluka. All the six Darsanas appear to have assumed concrete shapes as systems of philosophy during the period 200 B.C. to 300 A.D.

According to Sankhya philosophy there are two Realities in this vast universe of ours, the Purusa and the Prakriti. They correspond to spirit and matter or 'Chatanya' and 'Jada' but not exactly. Purusa is of the nature of consciousness (chit) but contrary to Buddhist philosophy it is a permanent or eternal reality and contrary to Vendanta it is not an all-pervading and all powerful unitary reality but there are infinite numbers of Purusas who are neither the creator of material world nor they are capable of any activity by themselves. Prakriti is of the nature of matter (Jada) but not quite so, as all physical change, movement and activity which is going on in the universe belongs to it not to Purusa and the exercise of the mental power behind all such activity also belong to it. However, such activity cannot take place unless Purusa and Prakriti cooperate with each other or unless there is union of these two realities. Purusa is light and sight of consciousness but it cannot move by itself like a legless man. Prakriti has active limbs for movement but is blind and has no sight for giving directions to its activity. Therefore, the entire world activity becomes possible only when the two realitie scombine.

With such combination the evolutionary process of cosmic activity starts but this requires some material to built up the world as it is. Three main factors, covering in a broad sense numerous elements, constitute such a material. These three factors, called, 'Gunas' are the 'Sattva', the 'Rajas' and the 'Tamas'. Sattva signifies what is pure, fine, good with an urge of buoyancy and happiness. Rajas signifies the feverish activity and restless race of this material world involving also its inherent pains and sufferings. The 'tamas' signifies what is static and solid which resists activity and involves an urge of lethargy and inactivity. When this three-pronged world material is at rest no activity takes place and then the world is also at rest or in a state of 'parlya'. However, when the three start working, the equilibrium which produces rest, is disturbed and the cosmic activity commences. The first product of this activity, as a result of the union of Purusa, with its light of consciousness, and prakriti, with its three Gunas, is called 'Mahat' or cosmic intelligence. Even as intelligence, 'Mahat' is counted within Prakriti, not on the side of purusa, even though in some puranas such as Matsya and Vayu Purana, it is compared to Brahman, who is believed to be the creator of the world. Mahat further transfers its intelligence to infinite number of individuals, and appears as 'Buddhi' or intellect of each individual. The 'Buddhi' in its turn gets knowledge of external objects through 'Manas' (mind) and sense organs and presents that knowledge to conscious purusa who is the subject in each individual. All experiences of outer objects belongs to Purusa but 'Purusa' itself being inactive, the experiences, come to it through an apparatus which is a part of Prakriti. The three main items constituting this apparatus are Buddhi, Manas and Ahankara (self-sense). No doubt ordinarily these three appear to be conscious entities, but here they are treated as part of prakriti. Also the three being of similar nature, they are indicated in Sankhya, by a simple entity called, 'Antahkarna' or internal organ. Of course Sankhya accepts that all the things of the world, come with 25 objects including the Purusa and Prakriti. The 23 other which are called Vikiritis of Prakriti are, Buddhi, Manas, Ahankara (3-5) five tanmatras of Sound, Touch, Smell, Form and Taste (6-10) five sense organs, Eye, Ear, Nose, Tongue, and Skin (11-15), five organs of action (16-20), five gross elements Ether, Air, Light, Water and Earth (21-25).

The Sankhya philosophy concerns itself not only with discovering what is the Reality in this world and what are parts of such Reality, but it is very much concerned also with, what is the objective of human life and how to achieve such objective. When Buddhi, Manas, Ahankara, all senses etc. remain on the side of Prakriti, the Purusa remains a higher and pure Reality. Not only all impurities, weaknesses, pains and sufferings of human life which are associated with Rajas and Tamas, but also joys and happiness which are associated with Sattva remain on the side of prakriti. The object of human life is to understand and have knowledge of this position and then break with the prakriti so that Purusa may get separated from weaknesses, sorrows and joys, and attain its higher position of Purity. This higher state is the Mukti or Liberation of soul in Sankhya and it is called 'Kaivalya', or aloofness. This state is not like the Mukti, in Vedanta or in other God believing philosophies in which the Atma joins the Paramatma who is all Truth (Sat) and all Bliss (Anand) besides being all-consciousness (Chit). Here the Kaivalya is mere aloofness of Purusa or existence of consciousness by itself for itself. As long as this stage of knowledge (gyan) about the distinction between Purusa and Prakriti does not arrive there in no liberation and the soul remains in Sansara or the wheel of births and deaths. Thus transmigration of soul as also the law of Karma, which causes the soul to fall in the circle of transmigration, constitute parts of the Sankhya Philosophy. But to reach the stage of knowledge which could end the Sansara, great efforts are called for and the individual has to practice certain disciplines. These are the eight disciplines of the Yoga philosophy of Patanjali, which are also adopted by Sankhya. In fact Sankhya and Yoga are treated as sister philosophies and there is much in common between them. The details of Yoga philosophy we will consider in the next chapter, but here we can only say that these philosophies are sincere human efforts to find out what is reality and truth, of course in the background already created by the two thought currents, one of the Upanisadic theism and the other of the atheism of Brahaspati's lokayata which subsequently came to be represented by Buddhism. The Upanisads with all their stress on the existence of Brahman, as the Self of man, also contains verses which exhibit doubt about such existence for instance verse 1-20 of Katha Upanisad reads "the doubt that arises consequent on the death of man—some saying, 'It exists and others saying 'It does not exist'—I would know this under your instruction. Of all the boons this one is the third boon". Here Nachiketa is asking a boon from Yama, God's power of death, but he gets the answer in the next verse number 1-21 reading "With regard to this even the gods entertained doubts in days of yore; for being subtle the substance (the Self) is not easily comprehended, O', Nachiketa ask for some other boon, do not press me; give up this (boon) that is demanded of me".

Such doubts existing in the Upanisadic text itself as well as the louder Buddhist assertions that there is nothing permanent, produced their inevitable effect in the minds of people who were at the job of constructing, the Sankhya philosophy. The latter were also feeling, as the Buddhists did, a great repulsion towards the belief of Vedic people, that Vedic texts possessed a divine authority following which they were performing with the minutest details the yajna sacrifices and other Karmakandas of Brahmna part of the Vedas, under the belief that such performance could bring about liberation of the soul or Mukti. The Sankhya protagonists did not believe in such Vedic authority and they relied on their own observation and inference. In fact the word Sankhya means reflection by human mind, and it was by this searching mind that they found the Buddhist theory also without any sense or truth, that there is nothing permanent and soul also dies with body. They therefore, held that Purusa was not only immortal but Pure consciousness. Sankhya is thus a step towards Reality and Truth even though quite evidently there are so many loose ends in this philosophy. One such loose end is what is that which falls in the wheel of births and deaths under the Law of Karma, when Purusa is Pure consciousness untouched by weaknesses of prakriti. The Sankhya answer is, it is Antahkarna, the internal organ, composed of the trio of 'Manas' (mind), Buddhi (intellect) and Ahankara (self-sense) and it is held that at death this Antahkarana survives as Linga Sarira (subtle body) and transmigrates. This would mean that Antahkarna is of the nature of consciousness even though in Sankhya it is a part of prakriti. Another loose end is who controls the Law of Karma and who causes the initials union of the two opposite types of realities, the prakriti and Purusa. Even though in the classical Sankhya theory there was no place of God but subsequently it came round to accept God as ideal Purusa. By its association with the disciplines of Yoga it also became nearer to accept the existence of God. Hence Sankhya is counted as one of the six theistic (astik) schools of Philosophy.

5

THE YOGA PHILOSOPHY

Yoga is one of the most famous ancient philosophies of India. As all Indian schools of philosophy are, Yoga is also basically a great endeavour to find out Truth and Reality about our world. It is, however, not merely explanation of the theory of Reality, and objective of human life as it has been able to discover, but it has become a practical science for development of a healthy body, which constitutes the instrument to achieve the life objective. It also concerns itself very much with the control of the instincts and wanderings of human mind so that a zone of peace and stillness, may get created therein which may be conducive to realise that objective. Mention of the word Yoga exists in so many Upanisads, like Katha, Taittiriya, Maitrayani and others as well as in Mahabharta, Bhagavat Geeta, books of Buddhism and Jainism. Gautam Buddha is said to have practiced Yoga before he achieved his exalted position as a world Teacher. Even though ideas about Yoga originated earlier than the Upanisads, wherein it is mentioned, it actually matured as a regular philosophical system much later, sometime in the second century B.C. when Patanjali formulated the Yoga Sutras. The evolution of the system, however, did not stop with the formation of Patanjali Sutras. Rather it continued to gather and align itself with other aspects and continues to do so even till these present times, but these are not integral part of the original classical Yoga of Patanjali.

Whereas Patanjali accepted without much change the metaphysical aspects of Sankhya, the latter adopted the physical disciplines of Yoga, and it is therefore, that the two are treated as sister philosophies. For development of body and mind Patanjali Yoga prescribes an eight fold course. The first is 'Yama' which implies restraints and they are 'Ahimsa' or non-injury to all living beings, 'Satya'—avoiding falsehood and practing truthfulness, 'Asteya'—non-stealing 'Brahamcharya' or absolute sexual restraint, and 'Aparigraha' or avoiding desire for more than the minimum essentials. The second is 'Niyama' which implies positive observances such as cleanliness both internal and external, Contentment, Austerity (tapa) and Devotion to God. The third is 'Asana' which imply postures of body that help to make the body fit for the function of a sound mind within. The fourth is 'Pranayama' which includes breathing exercises and the fifth is 'Pratyahara' or withdrawal of senses and thoughts inward from the outer objects. The last three are altogether for control and concentration of the mind. 'Dhyana' means steadying and fixing the mind on any object, 'Dharana' is to employ the mind in contemplation so that it becomes one with the object and the 'Samadhi' is the last stage of higher consciousness wherein the distinction between subject and object vanishes.

With all such elaborate disciplines of body and mind the Sankhya and Yoga do not much differ so far as fundamentals are concerned. Yoga like Sankhya accepts that the two realities are Purusa and Prakriti. They have not been created by any power like that of God, as is believed by Vedanta, but are self-created and eternal. The Yoga also believes that in the active world, as we see it, both Purusa and Prakriti must unite with each other to produce its activity. But because the ultimate goal of life is that Purusa must get free from all entaglements of Prakriti, the entire endeavour of Yoga discipline is to achieve the separation of Purusa from Prakriti. Although the word Yoga ordinarily means unity of two objects yet its aim is to bring about disunity or 'Viyoga' between Purusa and Prakriti. The liberated state of Purusa is envisaged not as union with the Supreme Soul of God, as believed by Vedanta, but altogether aloofness in its own Pure Self, as believed by Sankhya.

It will be observed that in the 'Niyama' part of Yoga discipline, 'Devotion to God' is stated as one of the observances. The fact remains that such devotion is not to achieve ultimate union with God, but God is envisaged here as a Perfect Purusa, which could be a fit object of devotion, among other objects of one's choice for concentration, in order to secure development of body and mind, the ultimate liberated state still remaining 'Kaivalya' or aloofness of Pure Purusa. Notwithstanding this indirect induction of God in Yoga philosophy, God is treated as the twenty-sixth entity of this philosophy, in addition to the 25 accepted by the Sankhya. Also because of this addition, Yoga is sometimes called 'Sesvara Sankhya', as distinct from 'Nirisvara Sankhya'. In Sankhya the stage of liberation of Purusa comes as soon as the knowledge dawns that Prakriti is separated from it, but in Yoga the liberation comes by active striving and applying the body and mind in contemplation and concentration.

Yoga accepts the Law of Karma and Transmigration of soul. The cycle of births and deaths goes on with its attendant pains and sorrows until the final liberation of Purusa is achieved. But when pains and sorrows of the world are a part of Prakriti, and Purusa is not subject to them, the same question arises here, as in the Sankhya, as to who suffers pains and sorrows of the cycle of births and deaths as well as the pleasures of the world. The Yoga answers that it is 'Chitta' which remains with the Purusa during its entire journey in different bodies in the course of transmigration. The individual 'Manas (mind), Buddhi (intellect) and 'Ahankara' (egosense) form part of Chitta. Thus 'Chitta', of Yoga corresponds to 'Antahkarna' of Sankhya. Yoga does not accept that any subtle body or Linga Sarira accompanies the Purusa during transmigration and 'Chitta' is not encased in any such body. However, Chitta's position is somewhat higher than 'Antakarna' as Chitta while in a body gets expanded or contracted according as the body is human or that of an animal. In this state of encasement in body it is called 'Karya Chitta' though still remaining a part of Prakriti which is not conscious. But on death in a body it becomes 'Karna Chitta' which is 'Vibhu' or omnipresent as a form of consciousness which is not material. Thus Chitta becomes nearer in nature to consciousness which is the quality of Purusa, while it is out of body but again becomes limited and attached to each Purusa as Karya Chitta while it is encased in a body. Inspite of all this, Chitta is a part of Prakriti and the objective of Yoga is to secure separation of Purusa from Chitta also to reach the destination of Kaivalya.

Yoga philosophy goes further to describe what happens to Chitta and Purusa when a cycle of the existence of the universe, as a whole, comes to an end and the state called 'Pralaya' sets in. In that state also uncounted Chittas continue to exist as part of the Prakriti. As they do not have any intelligence, being part of Prakriti, they are said to be having their individual ignorance or 'Avidya', Prakriti by its very nature continues to have its potential of activity and that results in a new creation. Such new creation thus comes into existence by the force of Avidyas of Chittas which in turn are part of Prakriti, and by the force of uncounted Purusas which again experience a fall from their Pure State. Here, however, God also has a part to play. That part is to remove any hinderance and clear the way for Avidyas to create the new world, because, God is with sight of consciousness while Avidyas are without any sight or intelligence. This aspect of Yoga is described by Dr. S. Radhakrishnan as "The Yoga Accounts for creation by the two agencies of God and Avidya. Through the force of the latter, the ever revolving energy of Prakriti, transforms itself into modifications as the mental and material world, while God, though remaining outside the pale of Prakriti, removes the obstructions offered by the latter"[1]. Darsanasagar Hari Das Bhattacharya also says about Yoga "It is time to remember once more that the object of Yoga psychology was to teach the way to self-knowledge and that to this everything else including devotion to God—was subsidiary"[2].

1. Radhakrishnan, Dr. S., *Indian Philosophy*, Vol. II, p. 343.
2. Bhattacharya, Darsanasagra H.D., "Yoga Psychology", *Cultural Heritage of India*, Vol. III, 1953, p. 89.

Such theories of Yoga involving in their scope, as they do, even the state of Pralaya, may not be readily acceptable to ordinary human sense. Yet Yoga philosophy is a brave endeavour and a big step on the journey to find out Truth and Reality. It establishes the existence of a permanent soul as Purusa as well as a permanent Chitta with each Purusa which together transmigrate in different bodies, as against, Buddhist philosophy which established that there is no permanent soul which transmigrates even while believing in the Law of Karma and transmigration of soul. As the race for finding out Reality has been advancing in the world, Yoga, as other schools of Indian philosophy, has brought in God to occupy a more central place than what Patanjali had originally assigned to Him. Yoga has brought in some Tantra practices as well, but essentially the system remains a science for physical development of the body and the psychic control of the mind.

6

VAISESIKA—NAYAYA PHILOSOPHY

As in the case of Sankhya-Yoga the Vaisesika-Nayaya are also two 'Samanatantra, or allied systems of Indian Philosophy. Their objective is also to investigate the Reality about the universe and to achieve liberation of the soul. Whereas Sankhya-Yoga are dualistic believing in two reals, Purusa and Prakriti, the Vaisesika-Nayaya are pluristic and are more inclined to adopt a scientific, logical and materialistic approach in their investigation rather than having a blind belief in any traditional authority. The origin of Vaisesika is believed to be by about sixth or seventh century B.C. but its significant development took place after Buddhism and Jainism had come into existence. Nayaya originated somewhat later than Vaisesika but this also developed as a post-Buddhist Philosophy. Both Vaisesika and Nayaya, on the one hand, do not accept the claims of Mimanskas that Vedas are divine words to be followed blindly for achieving liberation, and on the other hand, they refute the Buddhist view that there is no permanent soul and no eternal Supreme Soul of God. They ascribe the authorship of Vedas, not to God but to wise human beings, the Vedic sages.

Even though it has been possible to break an atom to discover therein an enormous amount of energy, it was Kanad Rishi, the author of Vaisesika, who first discovered in India that this world of ours is made up of tiny, atoms which he called 'permanus'. His atomic theory was further elaborated and interpretted through 'bhasyas' or commentaries by so-many of Kanad's successors, Parsatapada, Ravana, Bhardvaja, Vyomasekhara-Charya, Sridhara, Udayana, Srivasta-Charya and others. The word Vaisesika is derived from 'Vesesa, which means particular or distinct. Each atom has a distinct and independent existence, it is self-created and eternal. An atom as visualised by Kanada, is so tiny that one atom and even a dyad or two atoms combined, is not visible. Only a triad can be seen like a mote in a sunbeam. The single atmos are not further divisible and having their own distinct qualities they combine to produce the four types of elements, earth, water, fire and air. These elements themselves cannot be called eternal but the atoms of which they are composed, are eternal not subject to destruction at any stage. The fifth element of Akasa is treated as eternal by itself.

In opposition to the Buddhist theory that everything is constantly changing and there is nothing which could be treated as permanent and real, the Vaisesika held that nine real substances constitute the entire corporeal and incorporeal things of the world and these are, earth, water, fire, air, akasa, time, space, soul and manas. These real substances come under a category called 'dravya'. But there are other categories which are within human experience but cannot be called substances or dravya. Whereas the nine substances enumerated above can exist independently, the other entities are such that they are connected with and depend upon substances for their existence. The word 'Padartha' is used in Vaisesika to indicate all things which exist, can come within human experience and can be named. Such six 'Padarthas' cover the entire range of cognisable things and these are, Dravya (substance), Guna (quality), Karma (activity), Samanya (generality), Vaisesa (Particularity) and Samavya (inherence). Each of these Padarthas have further sub-divisions. For instance 'Guna' (Quality) is sub-divided into the following particular qualities (1) rupa (colour), (2) rasa (taste), (3) gandha (smell), (4) sparsa (touch), (5) sabda (sound), (6) sankhya (number), (7) parimiti (measure), (8) prthaktava (difference), (9) sanyoga (connection), (10) vibhaga (separation), (11) paratva (long time), (12) aparatva (short time). These qualities are connected with one or the other of the nine substances except the soul. The type of qualities which are connected with the soul are (1) Budhi (knowledge), (2) Sukha (happiness), (3) Dukha (sorrow), (4) Ichha (will)), (5) Dvesha (hatred), (6) Yatna (effort) etc. However, the concept of soul in Vaisesika is somewhat peculiar and different from that of Vedanta and other God believing philosophies. The souls in their natural forms do not have any consciousness, activity and knowledge. It is only when they occupy a body that with the help of mind and sense organs they acquire consciousness, knowledge and activity.

The cycle of creation and then dissolution of the world is an integral part of Vaisesika-Nayaya Philosophy as is the case with other ancient Indian systems except the Mimansa. When Dissolution comes, the four elements disintegrate into their atoms, which remain without any activity. The souls again become without consciousness knowledge and activity but they retain their previous sanskaras merits and demerits which cause their vesesa or distinctive nature. The 'manas' through which it gathered previous sanskaras, also remains with the soul in the Pralaya. The atmos and souls being eternal entities not subject to creation or dissolution, when the next creation starts they again form the basis of new creation. To the question what force causes the restarting of the functions of atoms and souls, the original Kanada's answer was, it was the 'Adrsta' their inherent invisible force or moral order. While Kanada did not originally bring the name of God in his system and it was, therefore, that the Adi Sankara criticised the system on this account, the successors of Kanada made good this lacuna. Besides the nine dravyas, they said Isvara is the tenth. It was Isvara also who willed the Pralaya or dissolution of the world and that was to give rest to the souls and other constituents. It was Iswara again who willed that the world may be created again and he gave the push to the atoms and souls at rest in Pralaya, to restart the creation. Thus even though according to Vaisesika God is not the creator of the world, in the sense that atoms and souls are not created by Him, He performs the function of the organiser and engineer by using the material of atoms and souls. In due course He becomes also the Controller of the world as Vaisesika-Nayaya holds that the actions of human beings are incapable by themselves to bring their rewards.

The ultimate liberation of the soul, according to Vaisesika—Nayaya Philosophy, comes only when the knowledge about the reality of dravayas and Padarathas dawns on the soul and its ignorance as well as passions drop down. The soul is thus freed from the bonds of Karma and from the cycle of births and deaths. In this freed state the soul rests without any feeling, volition and consciousness.

The word 'Nayaya' literally means reaching to a conclusion by reason and argument. The Nayaya philosophy is therefore, sometimes called 'Tarka-Vidya' or 'Vada-Vidya', meaning science of debate or science of discussion. During about six centuries before the commencement of Christian Era serious debates were going on in India about Truth and reality of this world. While Buddhism and Jainism were advancing their arguments against reality of God and against Karamkanda or Vedic rituals of Mimanskas, the six Brahmanical schools of philosophy or Darsanas, were refuting with greater vigour the Buddhist, Jaina and Lokayatas postulate that there is no God as also the Buddhist theory that everything is changing and momentry. In this background Nayaya developed as a science of debate and logic. The subject assumed such importance that all systems of philosophy needed its help for arguments and discussions. Its development went on in post-Christian era and has advanced even upto these modern times. Its history is deemed by some scholars to cover three periods, the ancient from 650 B.C. to 100 A.D., the medieval from 100 A.D. to 1200 A.D. and modern from 1200 A.D. onwards.

The Nayaya Sutras were written by Gautama, who is also called Aksapada. Commentaries on the Sutras and further commentaries on commentaries were added by Vatsyayana, Udyotakara, Vacaspati Misra, Udayana, Vardhamana, Visvanatha and others. A new school called Navya-Nayaya was commenced by Gangesa Upadhyaya in 1200 A.D. These authors have been carrying on the debate with Buddhists from whose side Dinnaga, Dharmakriti and others had been offering counter-arguments. The Buddhist defence, however, died down by the end of the tenth century A.D.

The first Sutra of Nayaya specifies sixteen topics which come under discussion in the philosophy. These are (1) Parmana, the means of knowledge, (2) Prameya, the objects of knowledge, (3) Sansya, doubt, (4) Prayojana, purpose, (5) Drstanta, example, (6) Sidhanta, accepted truth, (7) Avayava, members of a syllogism, (8) Tarka, indirect or corroborative proof, (9) Nirnya, determination of truth, (10) Vada, discussion to discover truth, (11) Jalpa, disputing angrily, (12) Vitanda, destructive argumentation, (13) Hetvabhasa, fallacious reasons, (14) Chala, quibbling, (15) Jati, false analogical arguments, and (16) Nigrahasthana, points of defeat.

Evidently the first ten of the above topics are positive ones and constitute the instruments to build up a valid proposition while the other six are negative and are such as can effect adversly that validity and should be guarded against. The first topic 'Parmanya' deals with approved sources of valid knowledge and such sources are of four types, (1) Partyaksa, perception, (2) Anumana, inference, (3) Upamana, analogy and (4) Sabda, verbal testimony. Through perception knowledge of an object is acquired when human senses come into contact with that object. Perception again is of two types, the indeterminate and determinate. At the first moment when an object is observed and its name and nature are not determined its perception is said to be indeterminate or nirvikalpa. Next when that perception is connected with the name it is said to be determinate or Savikalpa Perception. In this analytical manner all these four types of Parmanas and all the above mentioned topics are elaborately discussed in Nayaya Philosophy. This philosophy is thus attaching all importance to accurate definitions precision of language and right means of knowledge so that right conclusions could be arrived at about reality of things. Thus when Philosophers taking side of Buddhism held the theory of self-validity of knowledge, the Nayayikas held that knowledge must be subjected to verification by other means also and by the criterion of truth. Such emphasis on accuracy and truth of knowledge brought the Nayayikas in debate with some Vedantists also like Sriharsa and Chitsukha, about some aspects of Vedic knowledge which also needed verification for acceptance as reality. Inspite of all such concern for true knowledge, it is generally felt that Nayaya philosophy has gone too far in determining the ways and means of finding the Truth, but almost forgot to reach the Truth. It over-emphasised what kind of road leads to a destination but lost sight of the destination itself. It is, therefore, that Nayaya accepted the metaphysical aspect of Vaisesika while Vaisesika accepted the logical aspect of Nayaya. While each of these philosophies are incomplete by themselves, they make for completeness by combination.

By such a combination the belief of these philosophies in God got strengthened. While Vaisesika said atoms and souls lay in the state of Pralaya without activity and consciousness, the logic of Nayaya said they can't regain their activity unless some power gives them a push and that power is God. If Buddhist said soul dies with the body and yet they believe in the Law of Karma and Nirvana, Nayaya logic could tell them that this is impossible because without a permanent soul, who could get rewards of good and bad karma and who could achieve Nirvana? If Jainas said there is no God and yet they held that souls will suffer for their bad Karmas and enjoy the fruits of good Karmas, the Nayaya logic could clarify that without a Controller of Karma, the souls could not by themselves get rewards of Karmas and that Controller is God. If it was held by any Semitic philosophy that soul is permanent but it does not migrate in different bodies, the Nayaya logic tells them that new born children sometimes do express on their faces signs of happiness and sorrow and this cannot be unless they carry memories of their past lives. The principles of logic and accurate definitions involved by Nayaya are also made use of by Neo-realist European and American philosophers.

With all this, God neither becomes the Creator of the souls and atoms in Vaisesika-Nayaya philosophy, neither He is the ultimate object with whom the liberated souls rejoin in the state of Mukti or salvation. He merely remains a personal God who makes possible the working of this philosophy by removing the difficulties experienced by such working. Liberation of soul in this philosophy means its complete separation from body, manas etc. and complete cessation of activity and consciousness and to remain in a pure existence as if in a state of dreamless sleep. However, this philosophy is not clear about the relation of soul and manas, who suffers pains and pleasures and who dies and is reborn in the course of Sansara or Transmigration of soul. Uddyotakara held in his commentary Nayaya-Varthika that it is manas that transmigrates along with soul in different bodies but it is soul that experiences pains and pleasures.[1]

1. Radhakrishnan, Dr. S., *Indian Philosophy*, Vol. II, pp. 149-150.

7

PURVA MIMANSA PHILOSOPHY

Whereas Nayaya philosophy had indicated that 'Sabda' or verbal testimony, was one of the four Parmanyas, or sources of valid knowledge, the entire emphasis of Purva Mimansa philosophy is on 'Sabda' parmanya and the text of Vedas are treated as absolutely valid sabda parmanya. In fact the word Mimansa means the reasoning by which the deeper implication of the words of a text can be understood besides their obvious meanings. The word 'Purva' is attached to 'Mimansa' to indicate that this philosophy deals with only the 'purva' or the earlier part of the Vedas, constituted by Mantras and Brahmanas. The commencement of the Purva Mimansa philosophy can be taken as simultaneous with the commencement of the Smihta part of the Vedas, as the vedic Mantras mentioned various types of sacrifices and religious duties and it was essential to understand and interpret those Mantras for the purpose of performing those sacrifices and duties in an appropriate manner. Such interpretations and methods constituted the oral traditions which were handed down from generation to generation. They came to be recorded, in due course, in the Brahamna portion of the Vedas, but there they appeared in a disjointed and unsystematic manner. With the advent of Buddhism the Vedic Karamkanda came under Buddhist criticism, and it was found necessary to mould Purva Mimansa in a regular system of philosophy, dealing with the vedic rites and rituals.

The author of the Mimansa Sutras is Jaimini. who is treated

as a sage of fourth century B.C. As in Mimansa Sutra No. I-1-5, the name of Badarayana is mentioned, Jaimini is considered by some scholars, as a disciple of Badarayana, who is one of the authors of Mahabharta under the famous name of Maharishi Veda Vyasa, but this fact has not been established with any certainty. Sabra Swamin who lived in first century B.C. is the chief commentator on the Mimansa Sutras of Jaimini. Subsequently Kumarila Bhatti and Prabhakara who lived in about seventh century A.D. wrote their commentaries about this Purva Mimansa philosophy.

Out of the four types of sources of valid knowledge, the Parmanas, accepted by Nayaya, even with his sole emphasis on 'Sabda' Jaimini accepted the existence of the first three perception, Inference and Sabda, Prabhakra accepted Upamana or comparison also and added the fifth as 'Arthapatti' meaning presumption and Kumarila who lived somewhat later than Prabhakra added a sixth Parmana as 'Anupalabdi' meaning non-perception.

This Mimansa philosophy strongly holds that performance of Vedic rites, such as offering to deities, various kinds of sacrifices, the 'Yajnas' offering of oblations in sacred fire, the 'Homa' offering of charities the 'Dana' etc. constitute the most important duties of human beings and such duties constitute the 'Dharma' of man. Correspondingly the non-performance of such rites, as also performance of acts which are treated in Veda as 'Nisedha' such as killing a Brahmin, drinking of wine etc. are deemed as 'Adharma' or sin. Jaimini has held that performance of such rites is the practical aspect of all Vedic texts and Brahmna part thereof, embodying the details of these rites, is accordingly the operative and most significant part of the Vedas. The Samhita or Mantra part is just a secondary one as it only specifies the necessity of rites indicating the deities, to be worshipped, and according to him offering of sacrifices and oblations to them is the only practical way to worship them. For Jaimini the Upanisadic part, which has been ignored by him, is of no use from this practical aspect. All Vedic texts can be of five types (1) Vidhi or injunctions (2) Mantras or hymns (3) Namadheya or names (4) Nisedha or prohibitions and (5) Arthavada or explanatory passages.

The first type that is injunctions or commands apply to the text of Brahmnas detailing the performance of rites. Such texts, by their own intrinsic power, create two kinds of energy in a person performing the rite. For instance the text "Svarga Kama yajeta (one who is desirous of svarga) must perform sacrifice" firstly creates an impulse of avoiding lethargy and applying one self to action of performing the sacrifice. This constitutes 'verbal' energy produced by the text. The other is the 'actual' energy which is constituted by performance in practice, of the rite and which results in the achievement of svarga (heaven) in due course. The Vedic injunctions are also of three types (1) regular or obligatory the 'Nitya', (2) necessitated by certain occasions the 'Naimittika' and (3) Optional for achieving some boon or worldly objective the 'Kamya'. While Kumarila Bhatta takes all these three as the result of the Vedic injunction and accordingly coming within the definition of Dharma, Prabhakara counts as Dharam only the first two.

When Jaimini and other Mimansikas have attached such high and peculiar importance to performance of rites, in accordance with Vedic texts, their view about the authority behind these Vedic texts is also very peculiar. While Nayayakas who, as we observed, became believers in a Saguna or personal God, with limited powers, not having created the souls and atoms, held that Vedic texts consisted of words and words could only be uttered by some person and that person was God, the Mimansikas rejected this view. The latter held that there is no author of the Vedas and they are self-created. Jaimini has not mentioned God anywhere in his Mimansa philosophy. Neither his prominent successors like Sabra and Kumarila have made any specific mention about Him. They have not taken any cognisance of the words as uttered on behalf of God, in Bhagavad Geeta "I am verily that which has to be known in all the Vedas; I am indeed the author of the Vedanta and the knower of the Vedas am I" (Geeta XV—15), as also of the words in Rig Veda X-90-9 "From that God have sprung all offerings of oblations, as well as the Saman, Rig and other Vedas". In fact even the vedic deities to whom the sacrifices and oblations were intended to be made, have not been given any significant place in this philosophy. The entire stress is on physical performance of rites meticulously in accordance with the Vedic texts and that constituted the object of human life. Of course as in other schools of ancient Indian Philosophies, the omnipotent and omnipresent God, could not be altogether eliminated, and the later Mimansikas, held that the silence about God in this philosophy was due to the fact that Uttra Mimansa or Vedanta was to deal with that subject.

The Mimansikas justified their view about the self created nature of Vedas by the fact that Vedic rites were being performed from times immemorial but no one had associated the name of any author with such rites. Even when names of so many Rishis are mentioned as authors of the Vedas, the Mimansikas held that they were only interpretters and communicators to others but not authors. Neither did Mimansikas accept the theory of periodical dissolution, the Pralaya, of the world and its recreation afresh. For them the Vedas were beginningless and eternal. The knowledge contained in them in the form of Sabda pramana was the highest and infallible source of true knowledge, which did not exist in any other source in the world. Perception, Inference and other sources of knowledge were mentioned in this philosophy just to indicate that, not the knowledge obtained through them, but that obtained through Sabda pramana from the Vedas, was only valid and led to happiness of man. But the happiness is supposed to come after death when 'Svarga' is achieved through performance of Vedic rites.

According to Jaimini only the upper three castes are entitled to perform Vedic rites as Sudras who are not entitled even to study the Vedas, cannot perform such rites. Even the three upper castes who can perform the rites, have to wait for periods, which could be quite long, to get their rewards. This is so because the rites are performed at a certain points of time in one's life but the rewards in the form of 'svarga', with its accompanying happiness, could come only after death. The question arose who could ensure such rewards after such a gap of time with due regard to the fact that God is not accepted in this philosophy as the Controller of Karmas of human beings. The answer of Mimansikas was that the act of sacrifice or other Vedic rite carries a potency called 'Apurva' which remains with the Jivatman even after body is destroyed by death, and that potency persists until the results actually accrue.

So far as the nature of Jivatman itself is concerned there is no specific mention about it in the Mimansa Sutras of Jaimini. However the Mimansikas believe that Jivatman is separate from the body, the senses and the mind, and that the qualities of intelligence, volition and making effort for performance of Vedic rites belong to Jivatman. The prescribed rewards of such rites are also enjoyed by jivatman, though with the assistance of 'Apurva'. Even though Jaimini and his earlier successors, like Sabra and Kumarila, have not brought in God for any purpose in this philosophy, the later Mimansikas like Gagabhatta and Khandadeva held that even when God is not mentioned, it does not mean non-belief in God. Accordingly belief in God as well as in a jivatman, makes this a dualistic philosophy, as is the case of other ancient schools of philosophy discussed earlier. It is thus opposed to the Buddhist philosophy which does not believe in God and the authority of the Vedas. Accordingly the Buddhist code of moral principles is considered by Mimansikas as of little value because such a code amounts to 'milk put in dog's skin'.

Moksa or ultimate liberation of soul is also not specifically mentioned in the Mimansa Sutras of Jaimini. Here also later Mimansikas could not ignore this important aspect of human life. Kumarila Bhatta has made a mention of it in his work Slokavarttika that Moksa is not a state of all bliss and happiness but just extinction of all pain and sorrow. Happiness is experienced by jivatman in svarga as a reward of acts of Dharma which are solely constituted by performance of Vedic rites. Until all the rewards of Dharma are exhausted by actual enjoyment and those of Adharma are exhausted by actual suffering or annulment by acts of Dharma, Moksa is not possible. In Moksa the soul remains just in its natural state without any happiness or sorrow. Whereas the existence of a new force of 'Apurva' along with jivatman or soul is mentioned in this philosophy, no mention is made of anything like 'Antah karma' as in Sankhya, or 'Chitta' as in Yoga, which experience happiness and sorrows in the cycle of Sansara or transmigration, as distinct from the soul which in its pure form is stated to be free from such happiness and sorrows. No mention also exists about the Truth and Reality of the Universe as to who creates it and sustains it. Neither any other ethical values are described besides the Vedic rites which cover the entire scope of Dharma of man. Dr. Radhakrishnan therefore describes "As a philosophical view of the universe it (Purva Mimansa) is strikingly incomplete". Yet this philosophy, professing to be a practical one and upholding the highest, unchallengable and eternal authority of the Vedas has received a very important place in Hindu religion and the performance of Vedic rites still constitutes a fundamental base of religious life of Hindus.

8

VEDANTA PHILOSOPHY

Nature of Supreme Reality

Vedanta literally means the last part of Vedas which are the Upanisads. As we observed earlier the period between 11th Century B.C. to 6th Century B.C. is considered the Upanisadic period. The Upanisads, which are treated as Principal and authoritative were formulated during this period by lofty spirituality and deep intuition of various Vedic sages. Even when about sixteen Upanisads are treated as the main ones embodying sublime knowledge about Brahman, their number went on increasing to about 200 and so many of them could not reach the same spiritual heights as the others did. However the Vedanta Philosophy is based on the Upanisads, which are treated as the earliest and the greatest source of divine wisdom and knowledge.

The texts of the Upanisads, however, are not in a form of step by step running statements developing into any regular system of philosophy. Rather they are in the form of flights of emotion and spiritual longings full of deep intuition emanating from pure hearts of Vedic sages. The inner meanings of such texts are often not apparent and clear to common human understanding and sometimes they appear to embody contradictory statements. For instance Kena Upanisad verse II-3 reads "It is known to him to whom It is unknown; He does not know to whom It is known; It is unknown to those who know well, and known to those who do not know".[1] Similarly Isa Upanisad verse 9 reads "Those who worship 'avidya' enter into blinding darkness; But into greater darkness than that enter they who are engaged in 'Vidya'.[2] Only right interpretation can bring out the inner meanings of such Upanisadic verses. Interpretation of the Upanisadic texts is playing such a wide and overwhelming role that not only the various schools of Hindu Philosophy which claim to be theistic systems but also the atheistic schools of Philosophy such as Lokayata, Buddhism and Jainism quote one or the other Upanisadic texts in support of their systems. As a brief mention made earlier in Chapter on Sankhya, verse I-1-20 of Katha Upanisad reads, "This doubt that arises consequent on the death of a man—some saying 'It exists' and others saying 'it does not' I would know this, under your instruction, of all the boons, this one is the third boon".[3] Here the Upanisadic text expresses a doubt as to whether the soul of a dead man continues to exist or not and such verses are used by Lokyatikas and Buddhists in support of their theories that nothing of a permanent nature survives the death of man. In this verse the doubt was expressed by Naciketa before Yama, the god of death. Naciketa's father wanted to make sacrifice according to Vedic injunctions and he, with his son, was taking his cows to Brahmans. The son, however, realised that the cows were barren and his father will not get the desired reward for their sacrifice. Naciketa, as a good son, offered his own sacrifice. Yama was pleased with Naciketa and offered to grant three boons to him. In the verse quoted above Naciketa asked the third boon after he had asked the first two as happiness of his father and the Fire (or the means) that take one to svarga or heaven. But as Yama could not resolve the doubt, and grant the third boon as promised his reply is contained in subsequent verses from I-1-21 onwards. Verse I-1-21 reads, "With regard to this even the gods entertained doubts in days of yore, for being subtle, the substance (the

1. Gambhirananda, Swami (tr. by), *Eight Upanisads*, Vol. I, 1977, p. 61.
2. *Ibid.*, p. 18.
3. *Ibid.*, p. 114.

self) is not easily comprehended. O' Naciketa ask for some other boon; do not press me; give up this boon that is demanded of me." However the question by Naciketa and the answer by Yama in Katha Upanisad are treated as intended to test his suitability for the right knowledge to be revealed to him and the Upanisads do contain the answer that on death of man, the self which is non-different from Brahman does not die but continues to exist.

The bulk of Upanisadic texts are such which reveal the knowledge about Brahman or the formless spiritual (Nirguna) God, and the Vedanta Philosophy is constructed therefrom. From the Upanisads, however, Sutras were formulated initially as was the practice in the case of other schools of Philosophy, and 455 Vedanta Sutras by the great sage Badarayana, constitute the main exposition of Vedanta Philosophy. Most of the Sutras are again not any clear statements and consist of a few words leaving much scope for interpretting in different ways. Sankara's Bhashya or commentary on these Sutras is the most famous interpretation and it builds up Advaita philosophy. As we observed earlier (in the first volume), Ramanuja, Madhva, Vallaba and other philosophers have their own interpretations somewhat different from that of Sankara, even though they also rely on the Vedanta Sutras of Badarayana. Here we propose to understand the Vedanta Philosophy from the interpretation of the two great personalities who are counted and respected as highest vedanta philosophers, the Adi Sankracharya and Ramanuja.

In the first Vedanta Sutra Badarayana says "Athato Brahama jijnasa" meaning "Then therefore the enquiry into Brahman" indicating that Vedanta is essentially a philosophy about Brahman. The word 'Then' in the Sutra, however, can be construed to indicate that this philosophy about Brahman has connection with the previous philosophy, which is 'Purva Mimansa', as the Vedanta is also sometimes mentioned as 'Uttra Mimansa'. The first Sutra of Purva Mimansa by Jaimini reads "Then therefore the enquiry into Duty (Dharma)". As we observed in the last chapter, Jaimini has held that Brahmana part of the Veda is most important as it specified the actions, duties, yajnas and sacrifices which are sanctified as Dharma of man, by which he can achieve (svarga). Jaimini has also held that the Upanisadic part of Veda is of little use for that purpose. Sankra does not naturally agree with Jaimini and he says in his Bhashya on Vedanta Sutras "The special question with regard to the enquiry into Brahman is whether it presupposes as its antecedent the understanding of the acts of religious duty (which is acquired by means of the Purva Mimansa). To this question we reply in the negative, because for a man who has read the Vedanta parts of Veda, it is possible to enter on the enquiry into Brahman even before engaging in the enquiry into religious duty. Nor is it the purport of the word 'Then' to indicate order of succession; a purport which it serves in other passages, as for instance, in the one enjoining the cutting off of pieces from the heart and other parts of the sacrificial animal. 'He cuts off from the heart 'then' from the tongue, 'then' from the breast."[1] In Purva Mimansa Sutra 1-2-1 Jaimini had also said "As the purport of Scripture (Veda) is action, those scriptural passages whose purport is not action are purportless" but as indicated above Sankra has clarified that without attaching any importance to the injunctions of Purva Mimansa, the enquiry into Brahman can proceed on the basis of the Vedanta part of the Veda and this part has been treated by Sankra as of highest importance.

Sankara's advent took place in the seventh century A. D. and all the various sages and philosophers who preceded him and built up the different schools of Hindu Philosophy had treated the vedas as a whole, as the Sruti or revelation from God but had assigned importance to different parts besides interpretting them in different ways. However the one common purpose which was professed by all, including even the originators of heretic or atheistic systems, was to investigate what is the Truth and Reality of human life and the universe as a whole. In this common endeavour the Vedanta played an outstanding part and its contribution towards that

1. Thibaut, George (tr. by), *Vedanta Sutras with Sankara Bhashya*, pp. 10, 11-n.

common objective is the greatest. Sankra can be counted as the one philosopher, who has been the most loyal and faithful adherent to the texts of Vedanta.

If some materialist staked his claim to have found the Truth and Reality on the basis of what appeared to him the perceptible common human experience, Sankra was bold enough to refute that claim if it was inconsistant with the Vedanta part of the Vedas. The great Gautama Buddha had staked his claim to have found the Reality which he expressed in three main parts, (1) the perceptible material world is real, (2) the inner consciousness of living beings is real but only as long as it is within their material bodies and (3) that nothing is permanent in this universe.

Even though Buddha was otherwise a noble soul, having preached moral virtues, yet his philosophy being inconsistent with Vedanta, Sankara was bold enough to refute Buddhism by saying in his Bhashya under Vedanta Sutra II-2-32, "Buddha by propounding the three mutually contradictory systems teaching respectively the reality of the external world, the reality of ideas only and general nothingness, has himself made it clear either that he was a man given to make incoherent assertions or else that hatred of all beings induced him to propound absurd doctrines by accepting which they would become thoroughly confused so that—and this the Sutra means to indicate—Buddha's doctrine has to be entirely disregarded by all those who have a regard for their own happiness".[1]

Similarly Sankara in his Bhashya under the Vedanta Sutra II-2-33 refutes the Jaina doctrine that there is no reality such as the all-pervading Brahman even though the soul of jivas is a reality which expands and contracts according to particular bodies it assumes in the course of transmigration. Sankara also refutes emphatically at several places in his Bhashya, the Sankhya theory that non-intelligent Prakriti or Pardhana is the first cause of the creation of the world and that evolution commences when the Pursha who is intelligent but non-active cooperates with the Prakriti which is non-intelligent but active. Yoga does not deny the existence of God

1. *Ibid.*, p. 428.

but its concept of God is that of a perfect Purusa for the purpose of concentration of mind in contemplation, Dhyana and Samadhi, while as a twin system with Sankhya it adopts the same non-intelligent Prakriti as the first cause of the world. Yoga also along with Sankhya therefore gets refuted by Sankara. The Vedanta Sutra II-1-3 reads "Thereby Yoga Smriti is refuted" and Sankara Bhashya under this Sutra goes on to say "Although there are many smrities treating of the soul, all have singled out for refutation the Sankhya and Yoga because they are widely known as offering the means for accomplishing the highest end of man and have found favour with many competent persons.

Moreover their position is strengthened by a Vedic passage referring to them 'He who has known that cause which is to be apprehended by Sankhya and Yoga he is freed from all fetters' (Sve. Upanisad VI-13). (The claims which on the ground of this last passage might be set up for the Sankhya and Yoga Smrities in their entirety) we refute by the remark that the highest beatitude (the highest aim of man) is not to be attained by the knowledge of the Sankhya Smriti irrespective of the Veda nor by the road of Yoga-practice. For scripture itself declares that there is no other means of obtaining the highest beatitude but the knowledge of the unity of the self which is conveyed by the Veda. 'Over death passes only the man who knows him; there is no other path to go" (Sve. Up. III-8). And the Sankhya and Yoga systems maintain duality, do not discern the unity of the self. In the passage quoted (That cause which is to be apprehended by Sankhya and Yoga) the terms Sankhya and Yoga denote Vedic knowledge and meditation as we infer from proximity."[1] And indeed Sankara's interpretation gets confirmed from various verses of Upanisads and from one which is in the immediate proximity and reads "He is the one ruler of many who seem to act but really do not act; he makes the one seed manifold. The wise who perceive him within their self, to them belongs eternal happiness, not to others" (Sve. Up. VI-

1. *Ibid.*, pp. 297-298.

21). The words 'Not to other' refute the claims of Sankhya and Yoga according to Sankara.

All such refutation by Sankara of the various Indian Philosophies existing before his time, indicate that none of them had reached near the top of Truth and Reality even though they were great endeavours in that direction. Sankara's own interpretation of Vedanta Sutras and the Upanisads on which they are based, claims to touch that top and brings out the most significant Truth about the existence of One Supreme Reality that is Brahman. About the superiority of the knowledge divulged in the Upanisads, over that contained in the earlier three parts of Vedas viz. the Samhitas, Brahmanas and Aranyakas, Dr. S. Radhakrishnan also says "In the Upanisads we find criticism of the empty and barren ritualistic religion. Sacrifices were relegated to an inferior position. They do not lead to final liberation". He goes on further to say "The authority of the Vedas is, to no small extent, due to the inclusion of the Upanisads in them"[1] The Vedanta Sutra I-1-4 reads "But that (Brahman is to be known from scripture) because it is connected (with the Vedanta-texts) as their purport". This further confirmed Sankara's claim that the source of knowledge about Brahman is the Vedanta texts and Sankara's Bhashya under this Sutra I-1-4 is "It therefore is the task of Vedanta texts to set forth Brahman's nature, and they perform that task by teaching us that Brahman is eternal, all-knowing, absolutely self-sufficient ever pure, intelligent and free, pure knowledge, absolute bliss. From the devout meditation on this Brahman, there results as its fruit, final release, which although not to be discerned in the ordinary way, is discerned by means of the Sastra."[2] Besides the qualities of Brahman mentioned above Vedanta Sutra I-1-2 says "Brahman is that from which the origin etc. (i.e. the origin, sustenance and dissolution) of this world proceeds", and Sankara says in his Bhashya thereunder "That omniscient omnipotent cause from which

1. Radhakrishnan, Dr. S., *The Principal Upanisads*, pp. 49, 51.
2. Thibaut, George (tr. by), *Vedanta Sutras with Sankara Bhashya*, p. 25.

proceed the origin, subsistence and dissolution of the world—which world is differentiated by names and forms contains many agents and enjoyers, is the abode of the fruits of actions, these fruits having their definite places, times and causes, and the nature of whose arrangement cannot even be conceived by the mind—that cause, we say is Brahman."[1]

This Vedanta Sutra, viz I-1-2 is based on the upanisadic verses such as "That from whence those beings are born, that by which when born they live, that into which they enter at their death, try to know that. That is Brahman" (Taitt. Up. III-1-1).

It is thus observed that the Vedanta texts declare Brahman as the origin of this world, its sustainer and the cause of its subsequent dissolution, but Brahman as interpretted by Sankara, also being absolutely self-sufficient having no unfulfilled desires. He could not have desired to create the world. Sankara therefore maintains that Brahman did not have such a desire and origin of the world from Him is not actual creation. If the origin of the world, was called by Nayaya as 'Arambha' and by Sankhya as 'Parinama', Sankara called it 'Vivarta' or just an appearance due to illusion of Maya. The Brahman being above any desire and change and beyond the power of human mind to grasp its gunas or qualities such as Creator of the world etc., whatever qualities are ascribed to Him by human minds, they can apply to a lower form of Brahman, which is within the same state of Reality as the human mind with its Avidya is. This lower aspect of Brahman is therefore treated as within the Maya or world of human experience and is designated as Isvara. Isvara can be called the Creator of the world, its sustainer and ultimate destroyer.

The fact remains that various Vedanta texts and Vedanta Sutras do establish two aspects, one of the Absolute attributeless or Nirguna Brahman and the other the conditioned Brahman, or Brahman with attributes or Saguna Brahman.

1. *Ibid.*, p. 16.

9

VEDANTA PHILOSOPHY

The Nature of Self

Sankara held that Jivas, whose source is Brahman, are not different from Him but are the same in nature. This he based on the Vedanta texts, mainly the four, which are designated as Mahavakyas. These are "I am Brahman" (Brih. Up. 1-4-10), "Thou art that" (Chh. Up. 6-8-7), "This Self is Brahman'—(Brih. Up. 2-5-19), and "Consciousness is Brahman"—(Ait. Up. 5-3). However the obvious question arose that if the nature of Brahman is so excellent as indicated in the Vedanta texts, and which is also expressed as Sat-Chit-Anand or All-Truth, All-consciousness, All-bliss, how is it that jivas do not possess such excellent attributes but are involved in all types of pains and in the transmigratory cycle of births and deaths. Sankara replied that this was because the jivas do not realise their true nature that they are not different from Brahman, as they are involved in a state of nescience or 'Avidya'. But regarding this reply of Sankara, it can be said that if the jiva does not realise its true nature, we cannot say that Brahman does not realise its true nature because Brahman is all-knowing. Also if jiva is involved in a state of nescience or Avidya, Brahman is not involved in such a state of Avidya. How can therefore jiva and Brahman be the same in nature. In other words jiva or self is different from Brahman and this is just the opposite of what the Vedanta texts say. Sankara holds those texts as absolutely correct and therefore his explanation of this phenomenon is like this. When Vedic text says 'I am Brahman', whereas the Self is of the nature of all-pervading Brahman, but when it is in a body, it exists along-with that body and all that forms part of that body viz. the sense organs, the mind (Manas), intellect (Buddhi) etc. The body sense organs, mind, intellect etc. are not eternal and all pervading like Brahman but they are all unreal. Brahman is the only Reality and the Self which is not different from Brahman is thus the reality which is indicated as 'I' or 'Ego' of jiva. The body, sense organs, mind intellect etc. which are all unreal become 'Non-I' or 'Non-ego' and indicated by 'thou'. The Self as Brahman is the origin of all Creation and is therefore the subject while body, the sense organs etc. are the things created and are the object. The subject and the object or the Real and Unreal are opposed to each other like light and darkness but by a natural principle of Adhyasa or superimposition the unreal get superimposed on the Real and vice versa in the actual working of the nature. Sankara says in his Bhashya "It is a matter not requiring any proof that the object and the subject whose respective spheres are the notion of the 'Thou' (the non-ego) and the 'I' or 'Ego' and which are opposed to each other as much as darkness and light are, cannot be identified. All the less can their respective attributes be identified. Hence it follows that it is wrong to superimpose, upon the subject whose Self is intelligence, and which has its sphere the notion of the Ego—the object whose sphere is the notion of Non-ego and the attributes of the object, and vice versa to superimpose, the subject and the attributes of the subject on the object. In spite of this it is on the part of man a natural procedure—which has its cause in wrong knowledge—not to distinguish the two entities (the object and subject) and their respective attributes, although they are absolutely distinct, but to superimpose upon each the characteristic nature and the attributes of the other and thus coupling the Real and the unreal to make use of expressions, such as 'That am I' 'That is mine."[1]

When the attributes of body, the senses, mind, intellect etc.

1. Thibaut, George (tr. by), *Vedanta Sutras with Sankara Bhashya*, pp. 3-4.

which are unreal, get superimposed on the Self, the real, the jiva gets the feeling of a separate personality and begins to say 'I am Self' 'I' denoting here the separate personality subject to pains of the world and transmigratory cycle of births and deaths (Sansara), and 'That is mine', 'that' denoting here the worldly wealth, children, sickness, death, etc. The cause of such superimposition and the resultant feeling of a separate personality is the absence of true knowledge about the Real Self or Avidya and Sankara strongly advocates that the jivas should endeavour to remove this Avidya. When this Avidya gets removed the jiva acquires its true state of sameness with Brahman which the Vedanta texts mention as 'I am Brahman', 'Thou art that' etc. and this is the state where the jiva achieves final release and freedom from all pains and from the transmigratory cycle of births and deaths.

We have mentioned above the phenomenon of Superimposition, but we have yet to understand further its nature. Although Sankara holds the Vedanta texts as the most authoritative source of knowledge, he also accepts Perception or 'Partyaksha' and Inference or 'Anumana' as valid means of knowledge. Other Vedanta Philosophers added to these three 'Comparison' 'Implication' and 'Negation' also. But if the Vedanta texts hold that Brahman is the only reality while every thing else, the sentient and insentient world is unreal, should then the common experience of jivas by which they see and feel the world to be real, be altogether ignored ? In other words if through the working of Perception and Inference the world appears to be real, should it, still be treated as unreal? Sankara replies that the phenomenon of superimposition is necessary because without this the Perception and Inference cannot become valid means of knowledge and also several Vedic texts become meaningless. This is so because Perception and Inference presuppose the existence of a separate personality which perceives and draws inference. Actually the senses, mind, intellect etc. perceive and draw inference and they get superimposed on Self to produce the feeling of a separate personality. The senses, mind, intellect etc. in their turn depend upon a body and the body in its turn cannot work unless the reality of Self is superimposed on it. Thus the phenomenon of superimposition, which is another name of 'Avidya' or Nescience, is essential not only for the working of Perception and Inference but also for validity of certain Vedic verses which imply that a separate personality of jiva should perform good actions etc. to get their rewards. Sankara says in his Bhashya "We reply the means of right knowledge cannot operate unless there be a knowing personality and because the existence of the latter depends on the erroneous notion that the body, the senses and so on are identical with or belong to the Self of the knowing person. For without the employment of the senses perception and the other means of right knowledge cannot operate. And without a basis (i.e. the body) the senses cannot act. Nor does any body act by means of a body on which the nature of the Self is not superimposed. Nor can, in the absence of all that (mutual superimposition of the Self and the Non-self), the Self which in its own nature is free from all contact, become a knowing agent. And if there is no knowing agent, the means of right knowledge cannot operate. Hence perception and the other means of right knowledge and the Vedic texts have for their object that which is dependent on Nescience (Superimposition)"[1]

Accordingly Sankara attributes the feeling of separate individuality of a jiva, to the phenomenon of superimposition of objects which he treats as unreal over the real and vice versa. This feeling of separateness itself, he says, is erroneous and is the quality of Nescience, ignorance or Avidya of jiva. This negative quality has to be separated and dropped down from the jiva so that the realisation of Vidya or knowledge may prevail that Self and Brahman are the same.

Thus we observe that in Sankara's Advaita Vedanta the greatest stress is on three main points.

(1) Realisation of the highest aspect of Brahman as he observed and interpretted from Vedanta texts.

(2) Realisation of the Self as non-different from Brahman.

1. Thibaut, George (tr. by), *Vedanta Sutras with Sankara Bhashya*, p. 7.

(3) The realisation of 'Vidya', the True knowledge or 'Gyan' of the Highest Brahman, by which 'Avidya' drops down and final release of Jiva is achieved.

Sankara's exposition regarding (1) above we have already seen in the previous chapter. Regarding (2) above Sankara further holds that just as the all-pervading Ether (akasa) in the entire space and in the small jars, pots etc. is the same, similarily the all-pervading Brahman and the Self in a body, are the same. There is no separate soul which transmigrates from one body to another. Sankara says in his Bhashya "Really speaking there is no soul under bondage and different from God. Still just like the association of space with such conditioning factors as pots, jars, caves of mountains etc., it is assumed that God has association with such limiting adjuncts as body etc. And people are seen to use words and ideas based on that association, as for instance, 'the space in a pot', 'the space in a jar' and so on, though these are non-different from space. And it is seen that by that association are created in space, such false notions of difference as the space within a pot. Similarly in the case under consideration, the idea of difference between God and a transmigratory soul is false, it having been created by non-discrimination (i.e. ignorance) which causes the ascription of the limiting adjuncts body and the rest"[1]

In this explanation Sankara confirms that human soul is not different from God and there is nothing else which suffers pains in bondage. Evidently this explanation lacks clarification as to what suffers in the transmigratory cycle of 'Sansara' and who gets the rewards of human karmas.

1. Gambhirananda, Swami (tr. by), *Brahma Sutras with Bhashya of Sankracharya*, p. 51.

10

VEDANTA PHILOSOPHY

The way to reach the Truth

When Sankara so strongly holds that it is Nescience, lack of knowledge or 'Avidya' which is standing against the realisation of the high Truth of Vedanta 'I am Brahman', the question arises how can realisation of true knowledge of 'Vidya' be achieved. Sankara has mentioned the qualities of discrimination control of senses etc. but the main method for such realisation is that which is most common and that is full devotion or meditation on that Highest Brahman. It is abundantly clear from numerous Upanisadic verses as well as from Sankara's Bhashya under various Vedanta Sutras that worship, devotion and meditation should be on the Highest Brahman or the Self, the nature of which is depicted in those verses and in the Bhashya, and not on any corporeal forms, even though that Highest Brahman may be present and working as an all-pervading consciousness of those corporeal forms. For instance the Brih. Up. verse I-4-7 reads "He (Brahman) cannot be seen, for in part only, when breathing he is breath by name; when speaking, speech by name, when seeing, eye by name; when hearing, ear by name; when thinking, mind by name. All these are but the names of his acts. And he who worships (regards) him as the one or the other does not know him, for he is apart from this (when qualified) by the one or the other (predicate). Let men worship him as Self, for in the Self all these are One". Similarly another Brih. Up. verse, I-4-15 reads "Let a man worship the Self only as His true state". In his Bhashya under Vedanta Sutra I-1-4 quoted in the last chapter when Sankara depicts the nature of Brahman, he also says "From the devout meditation on this Brahman there results as its fruit, final release, which although, not to be discerned in the ordinary way, is discerned by means of Sastra". Thus we observe that even though in some Upanisadic verses Brahman is mentioned to appear in some form, and worship can be on Brahman with such form or as Saguna Brahman also, yet the Vedanta taxts as well as Sankara's Bhashya predominantly declare Brahman as formless and all consciousness, and that worship, devotion and meditation should be on that Highest formless Brahman. The Vedanta Sutras quoted below further confirm this position.

V.S. III-2-14 "Brahman is only formless to be sure, for that is the predominant note of the Upanisadic teaching".

V.S. III-2-16 "The Upanisad also declares Brahman to be consciousness alone"".

When Sankara quotes the Upanisadic verse "He who knows Brahman becomes Brahman" (Mun. Up. III-2-9) he on the one hand depicts the Highest aspect of Brahman based on Vedanta texts and on the other hand advocates that in order to know and become Brahman, devotion worship and meditation should be on that very Highest Nirguna Brahman and according to him that is the way to achieve 'Vidya' or 'Gyan' which leads to final release of Jiva. Sankara's Bhashya under Vedanta Sutra III-2-14 quotes several Upanisadic verses indicating that predominant teaching of Upanisads is that Brahman is formless and consciousness alone and he further says "Hence in sentences of this kind, the formless Brahman alone, just as it is spoken of by the texts themselves, has to be accepted. But the other texts, speaking of Brahman with form, have not the formless Brahman as their main purport for they have the injunctions about meditations as their main objectives. So long as they do not lead to some contradiction, their apparent meanings should be accepted. But when they involve a contradiction, the principle to be followed for deciding one or the other is that, those that have the formless Brahman as their main purport are more authoritative than the others which have not that as their main purport,".[1] It is clear that so far as the Truth about nature of God is concerned, it is this that He is formless and consciousness alone and Sankara definitely advocates meditation on such True God. However the need for meditation on some form, according to some Upanisadic verses, does sometime arise because some human minds may not be having the capacity to understand initially the True nature of God. In such cases the meditation on some form is only a stage to reach the worship of God but not worship of True God Himself.

However all this position about Sankara's Advaita Philosophy has given rise to another rather complicated issue. For the purpose of worship, the worshipper has to be separate from that who is worshipped. When the Upanisadic declarations are 'I am Brahman', 'Thou art that' etc., the Self is not separate from Brahman and thus there can be no worship. In this respect also Sankara gives the same explanation that the feeling of a separate individuality exists as long as the Self is in contact with or related to the limiting adjuncts of body, sense organs etc. and this constitutes the Avidya of jiva. In this condition of Avidya worship of and meditation on Brahman is possible taking him separate. Only when Avidya drops down the Self becomes the same as Brahman. In the state of Avidya, however, the capacities of intellectual grasp of all jivas are not the same and some jivas visualise Brahman with some form, involving a decrease in His higher real nature. Every form means some limiting adjunct on the High stature and magnitude of Brahman. Vedanta Sutra III-2-33 reads "For the sake of intellectual grasp (Brahman's magnitude is spoken of) just like the feet (of the mind or of space)". And Sankara Bhashya thereunder is "Hence it is (for the sake of meditation) that some magnitudes are merely fancied about Brahman with the help of changeful things. Not that all men can fix their minds steadily on Brahman, changeless and

1. Gambhirananda, Swami (tr. by), *Brahma Sutras with Bhashya of Sankracharya*, pp. 612-613.

infinite as It is, for men's intellects may be sharp, mediocre or dull". As indicated earlier, in this way a second lower aspect, that of conditioned Brahman or Brahman with attributes comes into existence, in certain circumstances for the sake of certain aspirants of Brahman who cannot easily grasp His higher aspect. But whereas the worship of Nirguna Brahman being of highest value according to Sankra, it brings about the knowledge of unity of Self and Brahman and final release of jiva, worship of Saguna Brahman is of a lower value and it results in the journey of jivas to the world of moon, the world of ancestors and minor gods and sometimes to the world of Brahman also. But in this last case journey to Brahman can only happen if the Saguna worship is also direct on Iswara and not through symbols.

The Vedanta sutras indicate the important principle that a meditation can fetch such rewards as one resolves as its objective. Vedanta S. IV-3-15 reads "Badarayana says that the superhuman being leads to Brahman only those who do not use symbols (in their meditation) since this two fold division involves no contradiction and one becomes what one resolves to be". Sankara in his Bhashya under it says "The teacher Badarayana thinks that leaving out those who meditate with the help of symbols, the superhuman being leads all others, who meditate on the conditioned Brahman to the world of Brahman Itself. For it involves no contradiction to admit this two fold division......for it is but reasonable that one who resolves to be Brahman should get divine glories of Brahman as it is stated in the text, 'One becomes just as one meditates on Him'. But one cannot have the belief of being one with Brahman when meditating with the help of symbols, since in such a meditation the symbol predominates".[1]

Sankara it is obvious, has all along been stressing the objective of knowledge or Gyan of the Supreme Brahman, so that by meditation on Him the Self may become non-different from that Brahman. Sankara seems to have made a unique endeavour that if Brahman was in perfect peace and bliss, the

1. *Ibid.*, p. 893.

jivas may rise from their state of pain and sufferings of the world, to that state of perfect peace and bliss, of the highest Nirguna Brahman. The Upanisads were there and Vedanta Sutras were there but it was Sankara who brought out from all that, rather not readily understandable scriptural material, the great Truth and Reality about existence of one Supreme Brahman, about His unique nature of Perfect peace and bliss and how that state of Perfect peace and bliss can be achieved by Jivas.

About four centuries after Sankara, Ramanuja, the second great exponent of Vedanta Philosophy, appeared on the scene of our world. Sankara and Ramanuja both accepted the Vedanta part of the Vedas as of highest importance and both relied on the Vedanta Sutras of Badarayana. Both accepted two aspects of Brahman, the Nirguna and Saguna but whereas Sankara laid all stress on Nirguna aspect, Ramanuja, on the contrary, laid all stress on a personal or Saguna aspect. Both accepted the Sabda (Vedas), Perception and Inference as right means of knowledge, but Ramanuja could not regard as unreal the world which those very right means of knowledge indicated to him to be real. He opposed that Maya and Avidya can conceal the Self-luminous Brahman and they can, as illusions, turn the real world into unreal. Ramanuja also held that neither could Self achieve such highest knowledge (Gyan) which could make it non-different from Brahman, nor by such Gyan, Avidya could drop off paving the way for final release of jiva. He advocated the way of meditation on God with love and devotion and that constituted the Bhakti marg. He held that Janana and Karma are means to Bhakti and from various Vedanta Sutras he derived the meaning of devotional meditation or Bhakti as the right way. For instance Vedanta Sutra III-2-24 reads "Moreover Brahman is realised in Samadhi as is known from direct revelation and Inference" and when Sankara himself said in his Bhashya thereunder "Moveover the Yogins realise during samradhana this Self i.e. Brahman, which is free from the entire universe of phenomenal manifestation and is supersensuous. Samradhana means the act of devotion, contemplation, deep meditation and such other practices, e.g. Japa etc". Ramanuja held that the samadhi with devotion, contemplation, deep meditation, Japa etc. all are indicative of Bhakti and that such Bhakti presupposes that Self and Brahman are not the same and Bhakti can be on the Saguna aspect of Brahman which is in easy grasp of human mind. According to him jivas as worshippers of Isvara are not only different from Him, who is worshipped, but remain different even in the state of Mukti after achieving liberation from the world.

In that state of release the jivas could be treated as in fellowship with Brahman but not merging in Him losing their own identity. Inspite of all these differences with Sankara, Ramanuja professed to be upholding the philosophy of Advaita Vedanta that there is one Supreme Reality not two or more. But when a question is raised that if souls are different from Brahman and possess separate individualities this makes a pluristic reality not Advaita, Ramanuja replies that Brahman is the single Supreme Soul while all the insentient objects and sentient beings in the entire universe constitute His body. The individual Self of a Jiva is just a mode of the Supreme Self in which it exists. This whole forms a Supreme Unity even with the individual souls therein retain their autonomy to act, perform Karmas and meditation.

As to the question whether all the four castes have the autonomy to engage in religious duties the Vedic Karmas and meditation, both Sankara and Ramanuja agree that Sudras do not have such entitlement due to the established tradition in accordance with both Sruti and Smriti. When the Vedanta Sutra I-3-38 mentions "And on account of the prohibition in Smriti of (the Sudras) hearing and studying (the Vedas) and knowing and performing (Vedic) matters". Sankara also observes in his Bhashya "The Sudras are not qualified for that reason also that Smriti prohibits their hearing the Veda, their studying the Veda and their undertaking and performing Vedic matters. The prohibition of hearing the Veda is conveyed by the following passages : 'The ears of him who hears the Veda are to be filled with (molten) lead and lac' and 'For a Sudra is like a cemetry, therefore (the Veda) is not to be read in the vicinity of a Sudra'. From this latter passage the prohibition of studying the Veda results at once, for how should he study scripture in whose vicinity it is not even to be read? There is moreover, an express prohibition (of the Sudras studying the Veda). 'His tongue is to be slit if he pronounces it, his body is to be cut through, if he preserves it'. The prohibition of hearing and studying the Veda already imply the prohibition of the knowledge and performance of Vedic matters; there are, however, express prohibitions also, such as he is not to impart knowledge to the Sudra and 'to the twice-born belong study, sacrifice and the bestowal of gifts".[1] Ramanuja agrees with Sankara in this matter as he relies on the same Sruti and Smriti texts as well as the same Vedanta Sutras.

But in regard to matters such as worship and meditation Ramanuja was very much influenced also by Visnu Purana and Bhagvata Purana. In Visnu Purana, Visnu's supremacy is depicted as unrivalled and in Bhagvata Purana worship of Krishna is adored. These exerted good influence on Ramanuja and the worship and meditation on formless Nirguna Brahman, which was the highest worship for Sankara, took a turn downwards to worship of the form of Visnu and his other various forms including that of Krishna. The cult of Bhakti on Saguna Brahman, or on so many forms of persons, who were treated as incarnations of Visnu, came to be started and preached by Ramanuja. Based on this new direction to Vadanta Advaita Philosophy, which came to be designated as 'Visisht Advaita' the Sampardaya of Vaisnavism came into existence as a wing of Hindu religion. Whereas the single Supreme Reality of formless Nirguna Brahman, which could not be split up into many and for devotion to whom, Sankara made all possible efforts in his life had all the potential to attract and unify the faith of all believers in One Supreme God, the Saguna Brahman, devotion to whom depended on particular personal forms set up for devotion and meditation, had all the potential to split up the faith of worshippers to those various forms and thus create many sects, sampardayas.

1. Thibaut, George (tr. by), *Vedanta Sutras with Sankara Bhashya*, p. 228,

etc. in a religion. This fact is actually evident in Hindu religion and even in the Vaisnavism as preached by Ramanuja, four different Sampardayas, Sri Sampardaya of Ramanuja, Brahma Sampardaya of Madhva, Rudra Sampardaya of Visnuswamin and Sanakadi Sampardaya of Nimbarka came into existence. Ramanuja wrote his own commentary on Vedanta Sutra of Badarayana which came to be called Sri Bhashya and he wrote also a commentary on Bhagavad Gita. His other works are Vedantasara, Vedartha Sangraha and Vedantadipa.

Ramanuja's new theory that Supreme Reality consists of Brahman as the Soul, while both the material part of the world as well as the individual souls therein constitute His body, further holds that such Supreme Soul is the efficient cause, while His body is the material cause, of the origin of the world. Thus the individual souls which are of the nature of consciousness and which Sankara held to be non-different from Brahman, become the material cause of the world. And keeping up his claim of being Advaita protagonist, Ramanuja also holds that these individual souls, while forming the body of the single Supreme Soul of Brahman, still retain their separate identity and autonomy which continues even upto and in the ultimate state of Moksa. This means that in the transmigratory cycle of births and deaths the individual soul carries its autonomy alongwith its good and bad karmas and Ramanuja says it is the soul which, as Karta (agent) and Bhokta (enjoyer) suffers the rewards of those Karmas. This constitutes another difference from Sankara who holds that soul being non-different from the all pervading Brahman, there is no question of its transmigrating and suffering the consequences of its Karmas. Who suffers such consequences Sankara does not make clear. Ramanuja's view in this matter, on the other hand, appears more clear but in that case the concept of the soul being permanently separate and independent to act, while forming part of the body of Brahman, is hardly consistent with the concept of Advaita. Radhakrishnan therefore found called upon to comment on this concept of Ramanuja "The distinction finally, that the Soul of God is the efficient cause and his body the material cause is untenable. We cannot take half a fowl for cooking and leave the other to lay eggs......unless Ramanuja is willing to explain away the immutable perfection of the Absolute and substitute for it a perpetually changing process, a sort of progressing perfection, he cannot give us any satisfactory explanation of the relation of the soul and of the Absolute to its body".[1]

Greatly impressed by the lofty ideas about Reality divulged by great sages and Rishis in the Upanisads and in the Vedanta Sutras, both Sankara and Ramanuja made most significant endeavours and dedicated their lives to achieve their objectives, but in their zeal to reach the Truth and Reality, in one way or the other, both went rather too far, crossing the limit of reason and possibility. Sankara depicted the nature of Brahman as so self-sufficient, so much in peace and bliss, that any desire to create the world was considered by him as disturbing His peace, bliss and self-sufficiency. In a way this was putting a limit on the omnipotent Brahman that He could not have a wish to create the world. Ramanuja went so far to depict the nature of individual soul that he held that even after Mukti it remained separate and independent, giving an indication that Ramanuja has come back after experiencing that state of Mukti. Such details and other information about the other world expressed by Ramanuja and the unique nature of Reality expressed by Sankara brings forth from Radhakrishnan the comment "Ramanuja's beautiful stories of the other world, which he narrates with the confidence of one who had personally assisted at the origination of the world, carry no conviction. Sankara's devastating dialectic, which traces all-God, man and the world to one ultimate consciousness produces not a little curling of the lips in the followers of Ramanuja".[2]

From ancient times humanity is on the march in search of Truth and Reality. Vedanta Philosophy is a great landmark in this march. Great sages and sears observed that when eyes were seeing, ears were hearing, tongue was speaking and so on, there was One intelligent Power behind all these. They observed

1. Radhakrishnan, Dr. S., *Indian Philosophy*, Vol. II, pp. 715-16.
2. *Ibid.*, p. 720.

that very single Power behind all nature because they had their hearts pure and open. They expressed the impressions falling on those pure hearts and these constituted the Upanisadic texts. The nature, however, is too vast and too deep that every Truth may become known to everyone. These texts were therefore diverse and varied with gems of truth scattered therein. Such ideas needed systematising and moulding into Philosophy and herein came the significant contributions of Sankara and Ramanuja. Considering only the positive side of contributions of these two great teachers, three main points emerge from the Vedanta Philosophy as of great value to mankind. Firstly that there is in existence One Supreme Reality of God. Whereas Lokayata, Buddhist and Jaina philosophies were groping in the dark not realising the existence of such Supreme Reality, the Sankhya, Yoga and Vaisesika had not proceeded even half way on the march in search of Truth and Reality, the Nayayakas and Purva Mimansikas did not have much concern with any Supreme Reality while framing their original systems, it was Vedanta which added its highest contribution about existence and nature of the Supreme Reality of God.

Secondly that the formless Nirguna Brahman is the highest aspect of the Supreme Reality.

Thirdly that meditation with love and devotion is the highest method to worship the Highest Reality.

PART II

NEW HEIGHTS OF TRUTH AND REALITY

UNIQUE CONTRIBUTION OF GURU NANAK

11

THE REAL GOD

Supreme and Perfect

As we have observed earlier it was in the lap of Shivalik range of great Himalayas, on a spot called the land of five rivers that about five million years back, the first sign of a civilised human existence appeared, when man began to walk on feet. Again it was at this very spot of land that about four thousand years back the melody of the earliest hymns of the earliest holy book, the Rig Veda, arose to vibrate all around. Then about three thousand years back the Upanisadic Rishis began to sing praises of One Supreme Lord, which spread all around the message that behind the various cosmic entities One Single Supreme Power was at work. The progress of civilisation, the quest into the Reality of Spirit as well as the scientific probe into the wonders of matter, have been advancing side by side in our world. A time was bound to come when all these three currents could get closer to each other and the whole Truth could come before humanity in a more integrated manner. Such a time did come about five centuries back from now and again on the same spot, the land of five rivers in India, appeared Guru Nanak on whom fell the great job of telling the Truth and Reality to the world in a more direct, more rational and more understandable manner. He said the entire Universe with its sentient and insentient parts, is the creation of One Supreme Power of God. While Sankhya-Yoga and Nayaya-Vaisesika, held the pairs of Purusa-Prakriti and atoms-souls, as self-created and eternal and Vedanta held that not the Nirguna God, who has no unfulfilled desires, but the Saguna God, Isvara, is the creator, the Sustainer and Destroyer of the Universe, Guru Nanak said the One highest formless God Himself is the Creator, Sustainer and Destroyer.

To emphasise His oneness Guru Nanak prefixed the numerical digit of One, right at the beginning of his Moolmantar, which describes the fundamental attributes of God. He said God is 'Ik Onkar, Sat Nam' as well as 'Karta Purakh', the former words indicating His unity as an all-pervading formless, eternal power while the latter describing Him as the Lord Creator of the entire universe. Suns, Moons, earths, waters, rivers, mountains, regions, glaxies, all sentient and insentient objects are created by Him. While God is Creator, man is a creature of God. As a created thing, man can never comprehend fully the qualities and nature of his Creator. Guru Nanak has therefore called Him as 'Beant' or limitless and unfathomable, not within full reach of human intellect. Yet God is what human beings, are able to understand Him. In his benevolence God Himself gives His own understanding to a certain extent, to those human minds who crave the same from Him with all sincerity, love and humility. To all such human minds God has appeared to be a source of all goodness but not a source of evil, and in this matter, amongst all sincere seekers, a common belief prevailed, at the time of Guru Nanak's advent. But this was not the case in respect of the belief about two aspects of God, the Nirguna and Saguna. It appears Vedanta Philosophy has depicted the higher Nirguna aspect of God as in perfect peace, without any worries and unfulfilled desires so that human beings worshipping Him may also become free from all worries and achieve a state of perfect peace and rest. And actually that philosophy has distributed human life in four parts, called Ashrams, the highest ashram being that of Sanyas, in which a human being renunciates the life of all worldly activities and worries and retires to a lonely forest abode for contemplation rest and peace, fulfilling the needs of his body by begging from house holders, or deploying his disciples for this purpose. Guru Nanak's philosophy on the other hand held that even when One God himself is the creator, sustainer and Destroyer of the world, His activity is all goodness and by such activity, He does not lose His peace as He is much above human nature. He could have desire to create and it is by His desire, (Hukum) or Will that He created the world and yet He is in perfect peace, tranquility and rest. According to Guru Nanak, human beings who worship such active God can acquire the quality of activity which is all goodness, and they should not run away from the active world but do honest vocational work, which is called 'Dharam Kirt' in his philosophy. 'Dharam Kirt' is essential for all able-bodied human beings while begging from others is rather a sin. Contemplation on God, while performing honest vocational work, gives more peace to human mind than running away from active world and depending on others for one's essential needs.

Saguna (or Sarguna) God in this latter philosophy means the immanent God who is present everywhere and in every living being. Immanence is not a second aspect of God but only a quality of the same One God who is both (Nirguna) transcedental and (Saguna) immanent. The Guru says "The Immanent and Transcedental is the same formless God who is in perfect peace and poise ; In His own creation He is appearing as Immanent".[1] Such immanence of One God makes all human beings equal to each other, as creatures of the same God and having the sparks of life, the souls, which have emanated from the same source, the Supreme Soul of God. But such presence of a part of the Supreme Soul in a human being with a perishable body, does not make him fit enough to be worshipped as Incarnation of God or Saguna God. Worship must be on the Supreme God Himself and accordingly whatever qualities or attributes of His excellent nature, human minds can think and realise about Him, apply to that One Supreme God, who is to be worshipped by all. However by a process of human thinking the Vedic Rishis split up One God into different aspects on the basis of His different qualities, described in the Upanisads, different names were assigned to those

1. Sargun Nirgun Nirankar Sun Samadhi app;
Aapan Kiya Nanaka appe hi phir jaap. (Nanak V—Sukhmani)

different aspects, and furthermore the different aspects split up human worship on different objects.

The Vedic scholars who have to interpret the Upanisads and derive a rational system of Vedanta Philosophy therefrom, have to indicate those different aspects of God, as are indicated in different Upanisads, and then they are at pains to prove that God remains One as an indivisible Supreme. Besides the two main aspects of God, the Nirguna and Saguna, the Upanisads indicate His other aspects also. Dr. Radhakrishnan while commenting on the Principal Upanisads says "The conception of tri-suparna is developed in the fourth section of Taittiriya Upanisad. The Absolute is conceived as a nest from out of which three birds have emerged viz. Viraj, Hiranya-garbha and Iswara. The Absolute conceived as it is in itself, independent of any creation is called Brahman. When it is thought of as having manifested itself as the universe, it is called Viraj; When it is thought of as the spirit moving everywhere in the Universe it is called Hiranya-garbha; When it is thought of as a personal God, creating, protecting and destroying the universe it is called Iswara. Iswara becomes Brahma, Visnu and Siva when his three functions are taken separately."[1] Having described these different aspects of God, Dr. Radhakrishnan makes bold efforts to uphold the Advaita Vedanta as a system of philosophy professing the existence of One God and he says "The Real is not a sum of these. It is an ineffible unity in which these conceptual distinctions are made. These are fourfold to our mental view, separable only in appearance. If we identify the Real with any one difinable state of being, however pure and perfect, we violate the unity and divide the indivisable".

The fact remains, however, that with such description of God in the Upanisads, Brahman in perfect peace cannot be Iswara, Iswara the Creator, Sustainer and Destroyer of the world cannot be called Brahman, Viraj remains distinct as manifested in the universe and Hiranya-garbha is distinct as the moving spirit in all sentient beings of the world. Brahma, Visnu and Siva were envisaged at some stage merely as the

1. Radhakrishnan, Dr.S., *The Principal Upanisads*, p. 66.

names of the three powers of Iswara, as the Creator, the Sustainer and the Destroyer of the world respectively. But they were also made distinct not only by treating them as separate personalities but also assigning a female consort to each, Saraswati to Brahma, Lakshmi to Visnu and Parbati to Siva. As we observed earlier whereas Sankara strongly stressed that human worship should be on Brahman, the Nirguna aspect of God, Ramanuja gave a complete turn towards worship of Saguna aspect and accordingly the three powers of God became separate minor gods alongwith the three goddesses as object of worship splitting up the worship of One God to worship of many minor gods. Obviously a minor god, in a personal male form, lacks qualities of motherhood and correspondingly a female goddess lacks qualities of fatherhood. Worship of such gods and goddesses is not worship of Real One God who is Perfect and Supreme in all respects. Worship of minor gods and goddesses does 'violate the unity of God and divide the indivisable'.

Guru Nanak said even if the three powers of God, those of Creation, Sustainer and Destroyer have come to be accepted by tradition, they should be treated, not as independent powers but as names of three qualities of One God. They should be understood as emanating from the same source. He says "There is One Supreme Power of God, which by its inherent nature, has spread all over the universe ; That power has come to be accepted as three subordinate powers ; One is the Creator (Brahma), another is Sustainer (Vishnu) and the third is one who, from his court of justice, passes orders for death and destruction (Siva); But actually that One God is running the show of the universe; His orders reign supreme; The great wonder is that the Supreme God is watching His own Creation, but the objects of the Creation, the human beings, are unable to see the Creator. My worship and reverence is to that Supreme God, who is beginningless, Pure, Infinite, Immortal and remains so in all ages"[1]

1. Eka maiy, jugat viaiy tin chele parvan; Ik sansari, ik Bhandari, ik lae diban: Jiv tis bhavai tivai chalavai, Jiv hovai phuiman; Oh wekhai unhan nadar na aavai bahuta ih vidaan; Ades tisai Ades,

Guru Nanak strongly emphasised that no form, no idol, no image whether of male god or female goddess can represent the fullness, reality and completeness of the One Supreme formless God. He therefore advocated worship of that Complete and Supreme God. The Guru says "We worship that one Complete Supreme God, who is represented by His Name; Nanak has realised that God and all should sing praises of that Complete and Supreme God."[1] If anything can represent God in His fullness, it is His Name, may be any name as adopted by His worshippers, but not any form.

We also observed earlier in Chapter on Vedanta, Sankara's explanation why in Vedanta worship of Saguna God sometimes becomes necessary because "men's intellects may be sharp, mediocre or dull". It is clear, however, that even for a dull intellect Saguna worship through a form, was to be an initial stage to rise to the higher stage of worship of 'Nirguna' formless God without which it could not be called worship of Real God. Even when a worshipper fixes his mind on a form, not the outer featuers of that form, its clothes and ornaments, constitute the object of worship but the inner qualities of that form. For the sake of latter the worshipper has generally to be in a state of 'antar-dhyan' and shuts his eyes to imagine those qualities and get inspiration therefrom. For worship of formless 'Nirguna' God also one has to be in a state of 'antar-dhyan' and use his mind to realise His qualities. Such direct worship of God is thus a perfect possibility. The practical experience of many centuries has amply proved the fact that those human minds which do not feel fit enough to contemplate

Ad anil anad anahit jug jug eko ves" (Nanak I—Japji)

Note : The word 'Maiy' in stanza No. 30 of Japji means 'Maya plus Ish' — 'the Lord of Maya' or 'Creator of nature', which is One God. The word does not mean 'mother' here. The three powers which are accepted by tradition are mentioned here as 'Chele' meaning 'subordinate powers' not 'sons' of mother. The word 'Viaaiy' indicates 'Viaapy' or has spread and 'Jugat' means 'method' or 'inherent nature' by which God is spreading all over.

1. Poora prabhu aradia, poore ja ka naon;
Nanak poora paaiya, poore ke gun gaao"
(Nanak V—Sukhmani)

directly on Nirguna Brahman and resort to Saguna worship, get stuck up at the stage of worship of particular forms and do not rise to the higher stage of worship of the One Supreme God. They do not generally realise God as an all-pervading spirit which is present in every human heart irrespective of his caste or creed. Such realisation is possible only through worship of the formless Supreme and Perfect God. Guru Nanak said all human beings can worship the formless God by singing His praises, contemplating on His Name and His qualities, which is a practical way to win grace and love of God. He puts the question and also gives the answer "What words one should utter to win the love of God; At the precious hours of this life, the ambrosial morns, remember God's Name and contemplate on his qualities."[1] He raised the banner of revolt against worship of forms and idols prevalent in the country of his advent and preached the direct worship of the formless all-pervading God. He held it unnecessary to split up God into two or more aspects of Brahman, Iswar etc. God is One, Supreme and perfect and worship of One can create One-ness, brotherhood and love among all human beings.

1. Muho ki bolan boliai boliai jit sun dhare piar;
Amrit vela sach naon wadiayi veechar.
(Nanak I—Japji)

12

THE REAL GOD

Without Birth and Death

The various theistic philosophies do hold that there is no known beginning of God and He is eternal and immortal. The monistic philosophy of Vedanta also holds the same but it says that the Self or Soul of man is not different from God. There are certain statements in the Upanisads which are called 'Mahavakias' and are treated as basic and most authoritative. Sankracharya and Maharishi Badarayana both treated these Mahavakias as 'Sruti' or words of God, being part of the genuine Upanisads. These statements are "Aham Brahma-Ami"—'I am Brahman', 'Tat tvam asi'—'That thou art', 'Prajna-nam Brahma'—'Consciousness is Brahman' and 'Ayam Atma Brahman'—'This self is Brahman'. It is understandable that the Upanisadic rishis discovered the high Truth that Brahman is of the nature of consciousness, immortal and present everywhere even in every human soul. They also discovered that human soul is also of the nature of consciousness, immortal which is not destroyed by death. Guru Nanak agreed with these Truths and said God is 'Akal murat' (Immortal), 'Ajuni and Sai Bhang' (without birth and self-created), but he did not agree that any human being could say 'I am Brahman', 'Self is Brahman' and that the Jiv-Atman, as it exists in human beings, is altogether same as Brahman. If Jiv-Atman and Brahman be the same, the question arises who performs good or evil deeds, who enjoys the pleasures of 'Svarga' (heaven), who suffers the pains of 'Narka' (hell) and who falls in the Sansara or the cycle of births and deaths, the transmigration of souls. As we observed earlier, the two great Vedic Philosophers, Sankracharya and Ramanuja, did not give satisfactory answers to these questions. Guru Nanak said that while creating a human soul, God added therewith a constituent which is called 'Haumai' or the 'sense of I'. This sense gives an individuality and separate existence to the soul. The soul alongwith this 'Sense of I' still continues to be one whole and of the nature of consciousness. The Soul ab-initio is a part of the Supreme Soul of God, but with a veil of 'I ness' over it, it gets a temporary separate individuality. This realisation of separate individuality is within the experience of every human being, just as a scientific truth. This realisation is upper most or outer part of the soul while the Pure Soul forms the core and its internal and eternal Reality. This individuality has not only been given a sense of separateness, but also a power of volition and action. It can therefore perform good or bad actions according to its choice or will.

This binds the 'human soul' or 'Jivatman' to the 'law of Karma' and consequential rewards of good or bad actions. It is under this 'law of Karma' that the soul falls in Sansara or the cycle of transmigration of soul. The entire purpose of human life is to suppress and ultimately remove the sense of 'Haumai' from the Soul so that it may become fit enough to rejoin the Supreme Soul of God, which is all light and from which it originally separated by the addition of 'Haumai'. In Guru Granth Sahib it is clearly stated—

> "When the Almighty God created human being, He added 'Haumai' therewith; It is that 'Haumai' which is subject to births and deaths in the cycle of transmigration of soul".[1]

The Vedanta statements 'I am Brahman' and 'Thou art that' can be taken as depicting the state of human soul before it assumed a body alongwith its 'Sense of I', the Haumai, or after it sheds the body along with that 'Sense of I'. But if Reality and Truth are to be depicted of the human soul, as it

1. "Jin rach rachia purkh bidhatai naale Haumai paaiy;
Janam maran usi ko hai re, oha aawai jaaiy"
(Nanak V—Rag Maru—G.G.S. p. 999)

actually exists in the living world, the philosophy of Guru Nanak fills up the gaps and states the correct position.

Before Guru Nanak the Semitic religions such as Christianity, and Islam also did not equate human soul with the Supreme Soul of God and treated the two as separate. They held God as God and man as man. But whereas Vedanta raised human self to become of the nature of Brahman, the Semitic philosophers brought down God to be of the nature of man, to some extent at least. For instance the Holy Bible describes in the Acts "But he (Stephen) full of the Holy spirit, gazed into heaven and saw the glory of God, and Jesus standing at the right hand of God and he said 'Behold I see the heavens opened and the Son of Man standing at right hand of God' " (Act 7-55-56). God had also appeared to and spoken to Prophet Moses as a man speaks to a friend and the Holy Bible records "And He gave to Moses when He had made an end of speaking with him upon Mount Sinai, the two tables of the testimony, tables of stone, written with the finger of God"—(Exodus 33-11 and 31-18). Thus God was seen in a personal form standing with Jesus Christ, speaking with Moses and writing with His fingers, as human beings do. Similarly in the Holy Koran, God is treated as a person when it is recorded therein "There is no private discourse among three persons but He is the fourth of them, nor (among) five, but He is the sixth of them....." The concept of God in these philosophies is thus more of an anthropomorphic nature and He is treated as a separate personality. Even though He is believed to be omnipresent and also omniscient knowing even the inner ideas of human beings, He is not equated with human and a relation, not of identity but of 'Otherness'[1], prevails between the Supreme Soul of God and

1. Dr. Mir Valiuddin says about such 'otherness'—
"Why do we regard the doctrine of pure identity as atheism and heresy? It is because to deny the 'otherness' of things means denving the Koran. If there is no 'otherness' between the Essence of God and the essences of created things, between the Creator and the creatures and between the worshippers and the worshipped, why then were the Prophets sent : Why was the Law (Shariat) imposed? Who are being commanded to live a pious life and do good deeds?. . . The Quran posits the essence of the 'abd' as 'other' and regards the essence of the 'abd' as a supplicant, a trustee a vicergent and a saint. (*Quranic Sufism*, pp. 115-117).

human soul. In Islam it is rather considered a sin of 'Shirk' to equate the two and human soul also remains separate after death and even while ultimately entering Heaven. In the Holy Quran it is indicated that after death human soul has to wait upto the Day of Judgment when its merits and demerits will be judged. By such judgment either it will enter heaven enjoying the pleasures as are enjoyed by human beings, which are mentioned in some detail in the Holy Quran, or it will suffer punishment in hell, in both cases remaining separate from the Supreme Soul of God.

Obviously enough if God is treated as omnipresent and omniscient, knowing even the inner ideas of human soul, it is not quite logical to treat the souls as altogether 'other' from the all-pervading God Soul. Also if Vedanta says that human soul is already God and can say 'I am God' (Aham Brahma-Smi), it is not clear what is the purpose of human life and what for is all the struggle to achieve Liberation or Mukti.

The Philosophy of Guru Nanak differs from both, the Vedanta as well as Semitic philosophies in this matter. As we have observed, Guru Nanak held that human soul is a part of the Supreme Soul of God but when God sent it to the world, clothing it in a body, He added with it another conscious part as the 'Sense of I' or 'Haumai', which gives it a separate individuality but cannot exist separately from the soul. The purpose of human life is to overcome this 'sense of I' by engaging it in good actions consistent with God's Will and ultimately to eliminate it, so that Pure Soul may become fit enough to rejoin the Supreme Soul of God and that means Liberation or Mukti. This 'Sense of I' as also mind, intellect etc. are not unreal or just as illusions only but, even not being eternal, they are real while existing as God created conscious entities.

If in Vedanta as interpretted by Sankra, Brahman being equated to Self of man, is expressed by 'I' as in 'I am God' and this 'I' is treated as the Real God, while other constituents of man such as 'Manas' (mind), 'Buddhi' (Intellect), 'Ahankara' (pride of I) etc. are treated as all unreal and are expressed as 'Non-I' or 'Thou', here in Guru Nanak's philosophy the position is reversed. The human soul alongwith its 'Sense of I' mind, intellect etc. expresses itself as 'I' while God is addressed as

'Thou'. Guru Nanak addressing the Almighty God and depicting His quality of Omnipresence says "O Lord Thou are present all over the regions of earths, oceans and spaces; Thy light is present in every Soul".[1] Sankra, as also his teacher Gaudapada, while interpretting Advaita Vedanta held Brahman as the only Reality, while all else, they said, is unreal and just an illusion. According to them there is no separate reality in the form of soul, with its mind, intellect, ahankara etc., which falls in the cycle of transmigration, and achieves ultimate Liberation or Mukti. Commenting on this aspect of Advaita Vedanta, Dr. Radhakrishnan appears compelled to say "The general idea pervading Gaudapada's work that bondage and liberation, the individual soul and the world are all unreal, makes the caustic critic observe that the theory which has nothing better to say than that an unreal soul is trying to escape from an unreal bondage, in an unreal world, to accomplish an unreal supreme good, may itself be an unreality."[2] For Guru Nanak the human soul with its 'Sense of I' is a reality along with its innermost core which is a part of the Supreme Soul of God. Great emphasis is laid in numerous verses of the Adi Granth, about the fact that every human soul carries the light of same common God, not by statements such as 'I am God' but by more rational and understandable statements such as "God is present in every heart.[3]

"The same God is present inside everyone and outside everywhere"[5] Guru Nanak never expresses the human soul as 'I am God' because this statement, besides being inconsistent with Truth and Reality, shuts off from human view the very purpose of human life.

Even though Guru Nanak divulged this description of human soul about five centuries back many philosophers of these present times are now realising this Truth. For instance Dr. S. Radhakrishnan while commenting on the Upanisadic statement

1. "Tu jal thal mahiyal bhar pur lina; Ghat ghat jot tumari" (Nanak I—Rag Blawal).
2. Radhakrishnan, Dr. S., *Indian Philosophy*, Vol. II, p. 463.
3. "Ghat Ghat mai Harju basai" (Nanak IX—Slok).
4. "Antar basai bahir bhi ohi" (Nanak V—Sukhmani).

that 'Self is Brahman' says "But that which is immutable and therefore immortal is not the empirical self. This transcedental Self is the Paramatman functioning in all minds. It is not capable of existing in the plural. There is only one transcedental Self and our empirical selves are psychical facts, streams of change. The jivatman is not a substance but an activity, whose nature is to change continuously. Whether we look at the real from the objective or the subjective point of view, the real can be defined only as a spirit. Though the being of man is spirit his nature is complex and unstable. There are other grades and kinds of life in the human individual". And he further says "Since it (Brahman) is apprehended by us, it is clear that we have in us a quality which apprehends it. It is we that possess the ineffable consciousness of the eternal. The soul it is that becomes aware of Brahman. The absolute is spirit. Though unspeakable in its transcedence, the Supreme is yet the most inward part of our being".[1]

The above words show that anyone who values Truth and Reality finds that the emiprical human self is not Brahman, even though that Supreme Brahman is the most inward part of our being. It is also found now that 'there are other grades and kinds of life in the human individual' while critically examining the Vedanta statements such as 'Self is Brahman'. Guru Nanak had divulged the Truth five hundred years back that there is in human individual a kind of life which he called 'Haumai' or 'Sense of I' alongwith the all pervading spirit of God. The word 'Haumai' might have been existing in Indian spiritual vocabulary before Guru Nanak, but it was he who gave it a significant meaning and described it as a positive constituent of human soul. In Vedanta negative terms were used as 'Avidya' or 'Ignorance', which prevented realisation of God and achieving Mukti, but these terms could not clarify as to 'Avidya' or 'Ignorance' of whom, if self is Brahman. The 'Haumai' or 'Sense of I' as divulged by Guru Nanak is a positive conscious part of human soul which can be both 'Kartr' or performer of good or bad actions and 'Bhoktr' or receiver of rewards of

1. Radhakrishnan, Dr. S., "Introduction", *Cultural Heritage of India*, Vol. I, 1958, p. XXVII and XXIX.

actions. Regarding this aspect of human soul Dr. Radhakrishnan also says—"It is this soul which reaps the fruits of deeds and survives the death of the physical body. It is the 'Bhoktr', the enjoyer 'Kartr' the doer. It is the Vijnana-Maya atma"[1] and this is in line with what Guru Nanak had divulged much earlier.

Bhagavad Geeta is treated as Smriti but it is held in great esteem as a divine dialogue divulging sublime knowledge about God and righteous duties of human beings. Its verse No. 8 of chapter four reads "For the protection of the good, for the destruction of the wicked and for the establishment of righteousness, I am born in every age". These words are of Maharishi Veda Vyasa who describes Lord Krishna speaking on behalf of God. God is without birth and death but here He is made to say 'I am born in every age'. The purport of these words is understandable that in every age God sends someone is human form but with His own blessings to spread His knowledge (gyan) in the world to protect the righteous and punish the wicked. These words cannot and should not be construed to change the fundamental nature of God who is without birth and death. But the fact remains that these words are by and large taken at their face value. God's power of sustaining the world, is first personified as Visnu and then so many are treated as 'Incarnations of Visnu'. God is thus believed to have taken birth in human form such as that of Lord Krishna and others. Anyone who is born in a human or other form, dies some day and has other limitations of a perishable body. But these forms are worshipped in Hindu temples as 'Incarnations of God' treating the verse 'I am born in every age' as authority, even though the Upanisads have declared that God is formless. Sankra has also emphasised that God is formless and in other verses of Bhagavad Geeta itself, Lord Krishna is mentioned as stressing the real nature of God to be formless and unmanifest not subject to birth and death. It appears a strange phenomenon of Hindu Philosophy that opposite and contradictory principles are all justified and practiced.

Guru Nanak stressed that no one with a perishable body

1. Radhakrishnan, Dr. S., *The Principal Upanisads*, p. 90

subject to birth and death is justified to call himself God or Incarnation of God to be worshipped as such. He emphasised that all human beings should realise the real nature of God as an omnipresent Spiritual Power whose light exists in every human heart. Such realisation of God has the effect of treating all human beings, with the light of same God, as equals deserving of mutual respect and love. In Guru Granth Sahib it is stated "One who realises the True nature of God, service and love of others rises in his heart like a fountain".[1] According to Guru Nanak service of others, help of needy, sharing of one's earnings with others in distress, is a far better way of worship of God than worship of images of 'Incarnations of God'. In Guru Nanak's philosophy God's real nature is thus preserved by treating Him as 'Akal Murat' 'Ajuni' and 'Sai bhang' that is without birth without death and self-created.

1. "Braham Gyani par upkar umaha" (Nanak V—Sukhmani)

13

REAL GOD

Sovereign, Just and Merciful

Guru Nanak then described God as 'Nirbhau Nirvair' meaning sovereign and just. God has fear of none and is absolutely free to exercise His Will, but He does so without showing favours or disfavours to any because even being sovereign He is perfectly just. The question arises if He is just to all, how is it that some are happy others in pain, some are rich others poor, some are intelligent others dull. How is there so much diversity. Guru Nanak says "In the midst of great Nature, God has made this earth a field for human beings to perform righteous deeds. The human beings therein are however of different hues and colours; Their names and forms are of diverse natures; This diversity is due to considerations of their own deeds; God is absolutely true and His Court of Justice is also true without favour or disfavour to any."[1] Originally when the human soul separated from the Supreme Soul of God and God added therewith a 'sense of I' giving it a will and capability to perform actions, it was of the same nature in all beings. The souls gathered diversity during their long journey of lives here on earth by their own good or bad actions. God is without enmity with any one and does not

1. "Tis which dharti thhaap rakhi Dharamsal;
Tis which jia jugat ke rang; Tinke naam anek anant;
Karmi Karmi hoe veechaar; Sacha aap sacha darbar (Nanak I—Japji).

make arbitrarily some high and others low. But if God is just and gives initially equal opportunities to all, human beings themselves should not arbitrarily make their own kind some high and privileged and others low and unprivileged. The Hindu religious philosophy has a prominent principle called 'Varna Dharma' which divides human beings into four classes. It is claimed that these divisions are on the basis of 'swabhava' or 'temperament' of human beings. Those who by their temperament are inclined towards mental and scholarly pursuits are treated as Brahmans, those having inclinations towards physical and administrative work are Kashatriyas, those inclined towards tilling of land, trade and other business vocations are Vaishias and those who have no inclinations towards any of these three types of work and are fit for work as menials and servants of others, are treated as Sudras. It is also held that this classification is natural and is existing in practice among peoples all over the world. But the hard fact is that no where in the world this division of human beings is given religious sanction as is given by Hindu religious philosophy. By such sanction this division has rather become a rigid division. By God given nature human beings do not remain unfit permanently for different types of vocations if opportunities are made available to them for such vocations and they get freedom to adopt any by their choice. But when Sudras are dubbed as unfit for higher vocations by numerous provisions of Hindu holy books, the Vedas, Smirities and Shastras, by and large this disability has come to be treated as by birth, not by temperament Such unfitness of them is treated as within the ambit of 'Dharma' or sacred law, and normal opportunities as human bings are being denied to them. As we observed earlier, the two highest Vedic Acharyas, Sankara and Ramanuja both held that Sudra are not entitled to study or hear Vedas. In the matter of the Hindu ceremonies of Upnayan and Yajnopavita the Sudra children are not treated like other children, even though by God's nature, children do not necessarily possess capabilities or disabilities just like their parents and often highly capable and genius children are born to ordinary parents. In the Purusa Sukata No. 10·90 of Rig Veda quoted earlier in Chapter 3, Brahman is equated highest as head and Sudras lowest as feet. Even when it is held that God whose real nature is formless, has no head and feet, yet these words are taken as symbolic and with divine sanction attached to whatever is recorded in the Vedas, Brahmans have come to be treated as highly privileged, while Sudras are treated lowest without privileges as human beings. What God has given to the latter has been snatched away by men. This is extremely unjust to these human beings who are condemned to a lowest humiliating position by man.

Guru Nanak raised a banner of revolt against these 'Varnadharma' distinctions also. He said human life is a most precious period for every human being to rise towards Gods, no matter whether he is of scholarly temperament or is fit for physical work. If God is perfectly just (Nirvair) to all, man should not debar any one from studying or hearing the contents of holy books. Everyone should have equal opportunities to join congregations of God lovers, sing His praises, meditate on His Name and do noble deeds to utilise this precious life to win Liberation or Mukti, which is the objective of human life. The Guru says:—

"The Kashatryas, Brahmans, Sudras and Vaishyas are all equally entitled to hear and act on the scriptural teachings. Anyone who turns towards God and meditates on His Name, can achieve Liberation from this world; Says Nanak the same divine spirit is present in every human heart".[1] In another place in the Adi Granth of Guru Nanak is recorded what Bhagat Kabir is saying to a Brahmin, "If you treat yourself a privileged Brahmin, having taken birth from the womb of a Brahmin mother, then why were you not born in a manner different from that in which non-privileged are born; If veins of my body carry blood, do thy veins carry milk instead that makes you privileged."[2] Kabir was a weaver of cloth and was

1. "Khatri Brahman Sud Vais updesh chaho varna ko sanjha, Gurmukh Naam Japai udhari so kal mai ghat ghat Nanak majha" (Nanak V—G.G.S., p. 747).
2. Jo tu Brahmin Brahmani jaaya, tan aan baat kahe nehi aaiya; Tum kat Brahman Ham kat Sud; Ham kat lahu tum kat dudh" (Kabir—G.G.S., p. 324).

treated as Sudra by Hindus as he has indicated in the above verse, but in the Adi Granth his sayings have been given a place of honour as is the case of sayings of Nam Dev, a printer of cloth, Ravi Das, a cobbler, and several others who by Hindu Varnadharma were dubbed as Sudras. In the Adi Granth they were made to sit in spirit along with the Sikh Gurus and the Sikhs bow to them in reverence. The only consideration was that these Saints were lovers and worshippers of One Real God whose true nature is described in Guru Nanak's Mool Mantar. In the Sikh tradition which developed by the teachings of Guru Nanak and his successor Gurus all are welcome in Sikh places of worship, the Gurudwaras, and in their common kitchens (Langars) irrespective of their caste or creed. Historical records of his time show that Guru Nanak befriended poor low caste men like a very poor carpenter Lalo by name, whom he called 'Brother Lalo' and spent time with him relishing his coarse bread and singing God's praises, while avoiding the nicities offered by a high caste rich man Malik Bhago.

Even though the Semitic philosophies of Christianity and Islam do not have caste distinctions like those of Varna Dharma of Hindus, but they do have beliefs that some human beings are shown favours and other disfavours by God. The ideas of original sin committed by ancient ancestors of man, Adam and Eve, coming on the heads of all human beings, the crucifixion of Christ as atonement for that sin and faith in Jesus Christ to become entitled for such atonement of sin, which are deep rooted ideas of Christianity, do indicate firstly that original sin comes on the heads of those who have not committed the sin, and secondly such sin is atoned from those who repose their faith in Prophet of Christianity but not from others. The Holy Bible says ''For there is no distinction, for all have sinned and fall short of the glory of God. We are justified freely by His grace through the ransom that Christ Jesus provided when God put forward as reconciling sacrifice through faith in His blood. This was for the vindication of His righteousness in forgiving the sins that previously were committed under God's forbearance and to vindicate His righteousness at the present time, that He is righteous and that He accepts as righteous him that has faith in Jesus" –[1](Romans 3-23-26). The Holy Bible also says "He who believes in the Son, has eternal life; He who does not obey the son shall not see life, but the wrath of God rests on him" (*Gospel of John*, 3-36). Similarly in Holy Quran of Islam, Sura III-31 reads "Say if ye do love Allah, follow me; Allah will love you and forgive you your sins; for Allah is oft forgiving, Most Merciful" Also Sura II-98 reads "Whoever is an enemy to Allah and His angels and apostles, to Gabriel and Michael-lo, Allah is an enemy to those who reject faith".[2] Even when Prophets of Christianity and Islam had the most noble object of projecting the image of God as all powerful and just, the way the scriptural provisions are understood, interpretted and practiced, both Christianity and Islam, do claim a superiority over other religions and also a privileged position to receive God's favour on the Day of Judgment.

Women, who as in the case of men, have also to achieve Mukti as the objective of their human lives, are treated in Islam, not equal, but having a status lower than men and so is the case of non-Muslims who as 'Zimmis' have to accept submission and pay Jizya as a token of their lower status.

1. Even Christian scholars, who value Truth and Reality, do realise that this Christian belief regarding original sin, is inconsistent with Divine Justice. For instance E.L. Allen quotes the views of St. Augustine "He (Augustine) therefore thought of Adam as an inclusive personality, in whose sin all his descendents to the end of time participated, so that even the infant, who dies at birth, has yet a share in the guilt of the first sin. Further the sin, committed in Eden, vitiated the whole nature of man, so that each individual is born predisposed to sin, and enslaved in will as well as burdened with guilt. From this condition only a divine intervention can save, and such an intervention must be irresistable as man cannot contribute anything from his side. Since as a matter of observation, all do not receive the grace that saves, God must choose to whom to give and from whom to withhold it, and since all are equally undeserving, the ground of discrimination must be sought solely in His sovereign Will. He elects, whom he will, to eternal life, and abandons, whom he will, to eternal death. That God is righteous even under these conditions, we must believe, how he is righteous, we cannot hope to understand." (E.L. Allen, *From Plato to Nietzsche*, p. 71).
2. Yusaf Ali, Abdullah, (tr. by), *Illustrions Quran*. p. 29.

The Holy Quran says "Women shall with justice have rights similar to those exercised against them, although men have a status above women, Allah is mighty and wise" (S. II-228).[1] And Sura IX-29 reads "Fight those who believe not in Allah nor in the Last Day, nor hold that forbidden which has been forbidden by Allah and His apostle (Prophet Muhammad) nor acknowledge the Religion of Truth (even if they are) of the people of the Book, until they pay Jizya with willing submission and feel themselves subdued."[2]

Guru Nanak made it abundantly clear that God does not show favours to any one on account of following a particular Prophet, Avtar or Guru. His straight theory was that God was absolutely just and all human beings were equal and none was of any lower status due to sex, caste, creed or religion. Advocating equal status of women the Guru says "Why should woman be treated as of lower status when even men who are treated as of highest status, the kings, are also born to women."[3] All should rise towards God with love and devotion to achieve Liberation as the objective of their lives. This theory was of a higher spiritual plane than that of superiority complexes on account of faith in particular Prophets and particular religions.

In his Mool Mantar Guru Nanak also describes the Real God as 'Gur Parsad' meaning that 'He is enlightening spirit full of mercy and bliss'. But a question can be raised that if He is perfectly just and judges human beings strictly by their

1. Dawood, N.J., (tr. by), *The Quran*, p. 356.

Note : It has to be realised that the words Women shall with justice have rights similar to those exercised against them" existing as a part of this Sura, do great-credit to the reformist spirit of Prophet Muhammad, as in the conditions prevalent in Arabia at the time of his advent women were having much lower status and they were treated as chattles of men and as slaves. But because of the fact that in Islam full equality of women with men could not be secured at that time, many Islamic scholars of these modern times are pressing for further reforms under the Islamic doctrine which is termed 'Ijtihad'.

2. Yusaf Ali, Abdullah, (tr. by), *Illustrious Quran*, p. 107.
3. So kion manda aathiai jit jamai rajan. (Nanak I—Rag Asa).

goods or bad deeds, where remains the scope for His mercy. The answer to this question is that if a person, at some stage of his life, beigns to realise, that his past life, full of evil deeds, was just a waste and advances towards God, sincerely repenting his past sins and seeking His protection, that constitutes such a meritorious act, that it can, by God's mercy, neutralise his past sins. God being full of mercy does bestow His forgiveness if one comes on the righteous path for the rest of his life.

The Semitic religious philosophies of Christianity and Islam also describe God as full of mercy and bestower of forgiveness on man and they are critical of the rigidity of Law of Karma as envisaged in the holy books of Hindu religion which existed before Christianity and Islam. But as we have already observed, the latter religions link up God's forgiveness with faith in their respective Prophets. If any human beings may otherwise be having similar merits on the basis of their good or bad deeds, those who repose their faiths in Prophets of Christianity and Islam do become entitled to concessions and recommendations of the Prophets on the Day of Judgment. In the case of Philosophy of Guru Nanak the only difference is that God, who is present in every human heart, Himself judges their merits and demerits for bestowing His forgiveness and no extraneous concessions are involved. The Guru has therefore said "God is present in everyone and is Himself aware of every things; He does not ask any one and Himself bestows His forgiveness".[1] God remains in this Philosophy, perfectly Just as well as Merciful besides having other fundamental qualities described in Mool Mantar of Guru Nanak.

The Mool Mantar was declared by Guru Nanak when he had reappeared after remaining untraced for three days while taking bath in river Vien at Sultanpur as mentioned earlier in Chapter eight of volume I. The fundamental attributes of God divulged in the Mool Mantar were preached by the Guru thereafter, throughout the world during his four long tours

1. "Sarb nirantar aape aap; Kisai na poochhai bakhse aap" (Nanak I—Rag Asa)

on all the four sides. As the Guru had said that he received a mission from God to spread His worship in the world, it is abundantly clear that inspiration to preach these attributes was from God Himself even though Guru Nanak did not say that these were the words uttered by God or were dictations from some angel of God. These words are treated as 'Gurbani' or 'saying of the Guru' but with divine inspiration and His Will. It is therefore stated in the Adi Granth "This 'bani' has come from God; It removes all worries of the world."[1] Thus here in this philosophy, the nature of God is projected with His attributes touching the highest Truth and Reality and here is one of the greatest endeavours ever made by any one, to spread worship of such Real God in order to remove the troubles and worries of this world and bringing about instead conditions of peace, brotherhood and love amongst mankind.

1. "Dhur ki bani aaiy; Tin sagli chint mitaiy" (Nanak V, G.G.S., p. 628).

14

THE REAL EVIL

What is the Reality about the source of Evil when God is altogether goodness ? Has Guru Nanak something new to divulge in this matter also to what the various religious philosophies existing before his advent, were believing ? The answer is in the affirmative. No outside personality or power comes to misguide human beings towards Evil according to Guru Nanak. Hinduism had so many schools of Philosophy, Advait, Visisht Advait, Dwait, Pluristic etc. but all believed in a power called 'Maya' which becomes a source of evil. Maya carries in those philosophies a number of meanings. The entire universe of forms, the Prakriti created by the formless (amurtha) God, is treated as Maya. When human mind is unable to explain the how and why of cosmic wonders and phenomena these are explained as visions of Maya. Maya is also treated as shroud of false appearance of illusion covering the Reality of God. The simplest meaning of Maya is taken as the various forms of wealth and attractive things of the world in which human mind is entangled, thus leading it astray from God.

Juduism and Christianity believe in the existence of Satan as the Power which misleads human beings towards evil. The Bible contains the well known description how Satan in the form of a serpent misled Eve and Adam to eat the forbidden fruit which constituted the original sin of mankind. As mentioned earlier, in spreading the Christian Philosophy the missionaries project a great point of its superiority that by his crucifixion Jesus Christ has effaced that original sin from those who repose their faith in him. No rational mind can understand how such a sin comes on the heads of those who have not committed that sin, but there is another declaration of Jesus Christ which clearly establishes the responsibility of human beings themselves for their own deeds. The Holy Bible says "What comes out of a man is what defiles a man. For from within the heart of man, come evil thoughts, unchastity, theft, murder, adultery, greed, wickedness, deceit, licentousness, vicious, envy, blasphemy, pride, foolishness. All these wicked things come from the inside and defile a man" (Mark 7-20-23). Evidently the description of Satan as a personified evil force, Garden of Eden, Adam and Eve, Original sin, are all symbolic descriptions, to bring home to human beings the existence of a strong Evil Force from which Jesus Christ wanted them to be saved.

The religion of Islam believes, a superhuman celestial personality of 'Iblis' as a power which misleads human beings astray from God towards Evil. But this personified Evil also appears to be a symbolic presentation to assist human understanding that an Evil force definitely exists in the world. It has, however, arrived at the same ultimate Truth that man himself is responsible for his evil deeds, but not without encountering much difficulty in its path to reach this conclusion. This is so because the two principles of the Source of evil and 'Predestination' are indicated in the Holy Quran in somewhat specific terms. Regarding the former it says "God misleads whom He wills and whom He wills guides or puts in the right path" (Sura 35-8). Going by its literal meanings, if God misleads man towards evil, man should not be subjected to horrible punishments of the hell, neither he should be allowed the pleasures of paradise if he treaded the evil or right path, as the case may be, not by his own free will but by God's Will. It seems however that this verse can only imply the overall position that if the entire universe is the creation of God, both good and evil existing therein, have originated from His Will. And there are other verses in the Quran such as "Surely we have shown him the way, he may accept or reject" (Sura

76-2-3), which do indicate that man as a created thing of God, has also been given a free will either to accept or reject the right path. Regarding the principle of Pre-destination the Quran says "Verily all things have been created by decree and everything they do is in the Books" (Sura 54-49). According to this verse all actions of man here in this world are already recorded in the Books or Tables of God. This also does not appear to leave any scope for free will of man.

But as we observed earlier human souls are treated in Islam differently than in Hinduism. Whereas the latter treats it as a part of the Supreme Soul of God, the former describes it as 'Other' than God. The 'Otherness' of human soul does imply its power to act in ways other than God's commandment. The evil actions of man are therefore explained in a number of ways. In Wasiyat Ali Hanifa it is explained "The category of sinful actions is not in accordance with Allah's commandment, yet in accordance with His Will ; Not in accordance with His desire, yet in accordance with His decision; Not in accordance with His good pleasure, yet in accordance with His Creation; Not in accordance with His guidance. In accordance with His abondoning and His knowledge, yet not in accordance with His intimate awareness or with His writing on the preserved Table".[1] Similarly Dr. Mir Valiuddin explains "Now again think over the 'existences' of things. These are manifest because of the immanance of the being of God in them. They are the manifestations, God is manifest in them. The relations, actions and states which appear in the manifestations, will be really attributed to God alone, they will be related to 'Haqq' (God). But in view of the manifest and the manifestations, two aspects now come into being viz. the aspect of being and the aspect of non-being. Evil and pain and ugliness which appear in the manifestations are due to their aptitudes and receptivity only. This is the aspect of non-being. The essences of things are relative not-being and not-being is absolute evil; Non-existential attributes too are all evil......Wherever Being's ambit doth extend good and naught but good is found, O friend. All evil comes

1. Bhattacharya, H.D., *Foundations of Living Faiths*, p. 389.

from 'not-being' to wit, from 'Other' and on 'Other' must depend".[1]

Guru Nanak did not recognise any outside power, real or mythological, as Maya, Satan, Angra Manya, Iblis etc. as the source of Evil. No serpent comes to any one to mislead towards evil. No celestial being like Iblis appears to anyone to ask him to commit an evil act. Nor does Angra Manya come to suggest that one may perform a wicked deed. Guru Nanak said it is the 'Haumai' the 'Sense of I-ness' in a human being which becomes in a way, the source of all evil that we see in our world. For instance some one while passing by a house, not his own, observes such a beautiful glooming flower, that his inner 'Sense of I' is attracted and he steals it away. Flower, by itself, is a gift of nature, it is a part of God's creation or 'Maya' and is not evil. The act of stealing is however evil and the cause of this evil is the 'Haumai' or the inner sense of man who says 'I must have it', ignoring the voice of his conscience that staling is evil. Similarly all the wealth of our world, the precious metals, gold silver etc. are not evil in themselves but become so when the 'sense of I-ness' in man covets to have them for self by means not consistent with norms of morality and spirituality or in other words by ignoring the voice of God which is also present in human soul and constitutes its inner core. The words 'norms of spirituality' used here imply that inner voice of God which is altogether goodness and virtue. Spirituality with its goodness is the foundation of morality. The structure of morality, however high it may be, comes tottering down, if it is not based on the strong foundation of spirituality. All created things of the world can be called Maya, and the philosophy of Guru Nanak accepts this nomenclature, but Maya by itself is not the source of evil. The Guru poses a question about Maya and gives himself the answer along with the question. He says "What is that thing which is called Maya and what actions are performed by Maya ? The jivatma is subject to pains and pleasures of this world because its Haumai (not Maya) performs all actions".[2]

1. Valiuddin, Mir, *Quranic Sufism*, pp. 144-145.
2. "Maya kisnu aakhiai kia Maya karam kamaae;
Dukh sukh ih jio badh hai, Haumai karam kamaae" (Nanak III—Sri Rag).

Of course 'Haumai' can perform both good as well as evil deeds which can bring the rewards of pleasures as well as pains, and it is thus of the nature of free will of man. Guru Nanak said God created the entire universe with its sentient and insentient parts. "All activity that is going on is within the over all Will of God; Nothing is outside".[1] But if God by His Will has given the quality of solidity to insentient stone, the quality of fluidity to water and air, and so on, similarly He has given the quality of exercising its will to the sentient consciousness of man which is represented by 'Hau' 'I' or 'Haumai'. "God Himself is Self-created ; He has spread all over, His formless existence, represented by His Name; Secondly He is the Creator of the entire universe, the activity of which He is observing with interest in a posture of perfect poise".[2] The I-consciousness of man is a part of God's creation and therefore a temporary one not eternal, as God who is the Creator of the entire universe, is also the cause of its destruction and ultimate dissolution. The 'Hau' or 'Haumai' being temporary second or separate from God, can worship Him and meditate on His Name. It can also go away from or ignore God and perform evil deeds. The entire activity of a human being is with this 'Hau' or 'Haumai' which gives it a separate personality and individuality. Guru Nanak has described in the seventh stanza of Asa di Var, so many activities which a human being performs involved in this consciousness of 'Hau'. Quoting a few instances he says "Involved in 'Hau' a human is born and dies", "Involved in 'Hau' one is full of Truth or full of falsehood", "Involved in 'Hau' one thinks what is evil and what is virtue", "Involved in 'Hau' one falls in Hell or Heaven".[3] It is abundantly clear that 'Hau' or 'Haumai' is of the nature of will of man which can perform both good and

1. Hukmai ander sabko, bahr hukam no koe (Nanak I—Japji).
2. Aapinai aap saajio, aapinai rachio Nao;
   Duiy kudrat saajiae, kar asan dithho chaao" (Nanak I—Asa-di-Var).
3. "Hau wich Jamia, Hau wich moa,...
   Hau wich sachiar kooriar,
   Hau wich paap pun veechar.
   Hau wich Narak Surag Avtar"
   (Nanak I—Asa di Var—G.G.S., p. 463).

evil deeds, make him full of truth or falsehood take him to hell or heaven, and so on. But when it performs good deeds, such deeds, are consistent with God's Will (Hukam), as God is the source of all goodness, and in such a case the higher God's Will is said to prevail not human Will or 'Haumai', Guru Nanak therefore says : "If, while performing any deeds, one understands and acts according to God's Will; Then no one can say 'Haumai' is asserted".[1] But in performing any deeds, if God's Will, which is also present inside everyone as voice of his conscience, is ignored, such deeds are evil ones performed by 'Haumai'. 'Haumai' thus becomes source of evil and suffers pains and sorrows as also bondage in the circle of births and deaths. It is therefore that 'Haumai' is more prominently associated with evil deeds and its subdual and ultimate elimination is very strongly and repeatedly stressed in the holy scripture of Guru Granth Sahib. In fact its elimination from the Pure Soul, which is the inner core of human consciousness, makes the Soul fit enough to rejoin or merge in the Supreme Soul of God, from which it had separated to become jivatman. Every evil act performed by 'Haumai', ignoring God's Will, goes on thickening and darkening the veil or curtain standing between jivatman and the all-pervading Param-atman. Mukti or Liberation comes when this curtain of 'Haumai' is eliminated and this constitutes the very purpose of human life. The inner voice of Pure Soul always warns human being not to indulge in evil but because a human is apt to ignore that voice, Guru's word or 'Shabad' is necessary to tell human beings what is evil to be avoided. This whole position about 'Haumai' is further confirmed when the Guru says "Haumai is the very personality of a human being; It is Haumai that performs all actions ; By performing evil deeds Haumai becomes in bondage and falls in the circle of births and deaths : But wherefrom Haumai originates and how can it be eliminated ; It originates by God's Will (Hukam) and its presence in human beings causes their actions ; Haumai is a serious malady but its remedy also lies in itself; By His grace

1. Nanak Hukmai je bujhai, ta 'Haumai' kahe na koe (Nanak I—Japji).

one seeks guidance of words of a True Guru and performs actions accordingly ; Says Nanak, hear ye all, this is the way to eliminate the sufferings caused by Haumai".[1] God is absolutely just (Nirvair) according to Guru Nanak, and He does not exercise His Will arbitrarily. It is not by His Will that some human beings are in pleasure and others in pain. Pleasures and pains of life come to human beings according to good or evil actions performed by their I-Will or Haumai. Of course God is controller of Law of Karma and He arranges rewards of actions performed by human beings in this and previous lives ; To this extent He becomes the cause of pleasures and pains of human lives, and the freedom of human Will or Haumai gets limited to the same extent. Thus all activity that is going on in the universe is by two Wills, the overall higher Will of God and the lower limited Will of jivas, the Haumai. Mind (Manas), Intellect (Budhi), 'Pride of Self' (ahankara) are all parts of 'Haumai'. Haumai as a remedy can

1. Haumai iha jaat hai Haumai karam kamae;
Haumai ihi bandhna phir phir joni paaih;
Haumai kitho upjai, kit sanjam ih jaae;
Haumai iho hukam hai, payai kirt pherahe;
Haumai deerag rog hai, daru bhi is maahe;
Kirpa kare je aapni ta Gur ka sabad kamahe;
Nanak kahai suno jano, it sanjam dukh jaae;
(Nanak II—G.G.S., p. 466).

Note: Some scholars interpret the word 'Hau' and 'Haumai' as indicating altogether an evil force. All actions performed by Hau or Haumai, they hold, are by ignoring God's Will and thus always evil. But as already indicated, if God has added 'Haumai' with Soul at birth of a human being and Guru Nanak said 'Involved in Hau one is born' surely 'Hau' of a child at birth, is not evil. Neither 'Hau' is evil when it is said 'Involved in Hau one becomes Truthful (Sachiar)' or 'Involved in Hau one goes to Heaven (Swarag)'. Also if 'Haumai' is altogether evil how can it be treated both as a malady of jivatman and also a remedy to cure that malady. Unless 'Hau' or 'Haumai' is treated as will of a human being, Law of Karma and consequential good or bad rewards of those Karmas cannot be logically explained. But regarding this Law of Karma, Guru Nanak has categorically declared in Japji 'As one sows, so shall he reap' (aape beej aape hi khah) and there are hundreds of similar verses in the Adi Granth of Guru Nanak.

take a jiva towards God but as a malady it more readily takes the form of Self-pride and Selfishnes. Thus it is Selfishness, as described in the philosophy of Guru Nanak, that has always been the real source of evil in our world. It was so in the past and it continues to be so in the present times. The Selfishness of a Rani of King Dasratha sent Rama to forest life. The selfishness of Ravana prompted him to abduct Sita, selfishness is at the base of the entire epoch of Ramayana. Selfishness between two families of Korava and Pandvas was at the base of the epoch of Mahabharta. In the present times Selfishness is rampant at every level. At individual level some people are rolling in luxuries but are selfish enough not to care for removing poverty and misery of others. At group level to achieve their selfish ends of seeing their groups and parties in a dominant position they do not hesitate even to commit murders and other evil acts. At the national level the world has become divided in two main camps, each of which is so selfish that in order to be counted as number one power, it is feverishly working to stockpile deadly nuclear weapons enough to murder and annihilate the whole mankind. Even at the level of religion people have become so selfish that to claim 'My religion is truest' 'My Prophet is highest' they are prepared to throw away all norms of morality and spirituality and resort to murder, plunder, demolishing religious places of others, dishonouring women and killing innocent persons, women and children. In the present times evil is speading its nefarious shadow all the world over and leading it to its doom of untold sufferings and miseries. The secular powers, the rulers are not proving equal to suppress the fast spreading evil, because they themselves fall a prey to selfishness.

The liberation of human soul or Mukti has been described by Vedanta and other Hindu systems of philosophies differently as we observed earlier. Sankra said the dawning of 'Vidya' or 'Gyan' (knowledge), that Self is non-different from Brahman, is Mukti and for achieving it, besides meditation on the Supreme Brahman, he has advocated renunciation of the active world of pleasures and pains, separating oneself from the entanglements of wordly affairs, as the way of great merit. In Ramanuja's exposition of Vedanta, Mukti meant reaching God through Bhakti or meditation with love and devotion, but here also the Vedic concept of renunciation of active world was of great merit for its achievement. According to philosophy of Guru Nanak the renunciation of active world carries no merit whatsoever. Rather it is absolutely wrong to run away from normal affairs and vocations of the world and become recluses. For achieving Liberation, what is to be renunciated and separated from the soul is its part of 'Haumai' the sense of I-ness and selfishness, which is the real evil.

But the important question is what is the way to subdue the 'Sense of I' or Haumai which causes evil. Guru Nanak has laid greatest stress that human beings should understand 'Haumai' as the real source of evil. Only if the real malady is rightly diagnosed, it will become possible to apply correct remedy. If Vedanta has raised rythem of a song 'I am Brahman', 'Self is Brahman' etc. Guru Nanak has stressed that in order to subdue the source of evil in man, human beings must turn towards God and raise the rythem of a song of 'Thou' and 'Thine' instead of 'I and 'Mine'. They will then be saying "O God, Thou are my creator' 'Thou are creator of entire universe'. 'Thou are bestower of all boons of life' so on. Guru Gobind Singh while dictating to a Sikh, Bhai Mani Singh, his famous composition, the 'Akal Ustat', once rose to such spiritual heights of ecstacy that he went on uttering 'O God it is Thou, Thou, Thou' so that sixteen pages were filled up by one word 'Thou'. Subsequently it was allowed to be retained recorded therein sixteen times only for the sake of brevity. Similar is the experience of some saints of God, whose compositions are recorded in Guru Granth Sahib. For instance Bhagat Kabir says "By saying Thou, Thou O God I have become Thou; No more remains in me my I-ness; When this I-ness which separates, is eliminated, I see nothing else but Thou wherever I see".[1] Similarly Bhagat Ravidas

1. Tu Tu Karta Tu bhia mujh mai raha na hun;
Jab aapa parka mit gia jat dekha tat Tu.
(G.G.S., p. 1375).

says "When I assert my 'I-ness', Thou art not ; But now Thou art and my I-ness is no more".[1] Guru Nanak has thus advocated this remedy of turning towards God, getting guidance of a True Guru, always keeping remembrance of God in our hearts, so that the goodness of God may subdue and eliminate the evil.

1. Jab ham hote tab Tu naahi;
Ab Tu hi mai naahi
(G.G.S., p. 657, Rag Sorath).

15

TRUE TEACHER

Full of Humility and Love

After seeking to understand what is the source of goodness and righteousness and what is the source of sin and evils we now proceed to understand what is the role of Prophets and Gurus in our world. In the Philosophy of Guru Nanak the role of True Teacher, expressed in simple words, is that he joins human beings with the source of righteousness, which is God, and he saves them from the clutches of the source of evil, which is 'Haumai' or selfishness.

Guru Nanak accepted the belief of previous religious philosophies that a human mind is weak in nature and it does stand in need of guidance from a True Teacher. Human minds flow more readily towards evil than towards righteousness. God is present in every human soul and whenever any one commits an evil act, the inner voice of God, which is called voice of one's conscience, does give a call to desist. But man, due to his weak nature, often ignores that inner voice. Another voice of a True Teacher thus becomes essential for all to get guidance in order that the darkness of Haumai may be removed and they may be able to rejoin the source of righteousness or the light of God, which leads to achieve the objective of human life. However for guiding human beings to God and saving them from the strong evil force of 'Haumai', it is most essential that the True Teacher himself must be fully competent to undertake such a great job. He should have the knowledge (Gyan) of God and should also be free from the serious ailment of Selfishness or Haumai. The Guru says "Only he can be called True Guru who has knowledge (gyan) of True God; By guidance of such True Guru a disciple can achieve Liberation; All praises are due to God, sing His praises, says Nanak".[1] The Guru also says "Haumai, as attractive worldly things (Maya), leads astray from God; It is not easily subdued nor its subdual can be purchased as a commodity of market: Only by a True Guru's words of guidance it can be subdued and eliminated; Then only human mind becomes pure and God's Name resides therein; Says Nanak this Haumai can be overcome only by guidance of Guru's words which a true disciple imbibes in himself and acts thereon."[2]

Subdual of the sense of Haumai in man is not so easy, in practice, as to say so. In the recent past several persons, perhaps taking advantage of India's past spiritual heritage, are calling themselves as 'Gurus'. Their field of activity is mostly the rich countries of Europe and America. They have been able to attract many rich disciples, whom they have been giving spiritual lessons by charging fees or otherwise receiving their offerings. In this way they have become so rich that they have been able to acquire in those countries palatial buildings as their Ashrams, and are passing ostentacious lives of luxury with costly cars to ride. These so called 'Gurus' are therefore not willing to make as their field of activity, their own land of India whose masses are not only steeped in poverty but are sinking lower in the values of morality and spirituality. In some of these rich western countries it has, however, now been realised that these spiritual Teachers are working for achieving selfish ends of gathering riches and at some places restrictions have been imposed on their activities. In fact 'Selfishness' and

1. Sat purakh jin jaania, Satgur tis ka naaon;
Tis kai sang Sikh udhrai Nanak Har gun gaao.
(Nanak V—Sukhmani).

2. Haumai Maya mohini duje lage jaae;
Na ih mari na mare, no ih hat bikaae;
Gur kai sabad parjaaliai, tan ih vicho jaae;
Tan man hovai ujla, naam vasai man aae;
Nanak maya ka marran sabad hai, Gurmukh paaia jaae.
(Nanak III, G.G.S., p. 853).

Spirituality are opposing forces and cannot go together in the long run. These modern 'Gurus' themselves not being free from this serious malady they cannot make their disciples free from selfishness even when the latter are offering large sums of money because spirituality and subdual of Selfishness cannot be purchased as a commodity of market.

The word 'Guru' literally means a Teacher. With this meaning there can be professional 'Gurus' such as those of music, sculptor, wrestling etc. but every body cannot become a 'True Guru' competent enough to guide human beings towards God and assist them to achieve Liberation or Mukti. Of course there can be some human beings with higher spiritual merits than others and they can be called 'Saints' 'Bhagats' etc. But the True Teachers, Prophets and Gurus are sent to the world from time to time by God Himself. As we observed earlier, Veda Vayasa appears to have intended to convey this divine phenomenon when he mentions in Bhagavad Geeta the words of Lord Krishna spoken on behalf of God "For the protection of the good, for the destruction of the wicked and for the establishment of Dharma (righteousness) I am born in every age",[1] God is without birth and death and His fundamental nature of being eternal and immortal cannot be denied by anyone. Whereas Maharishi Veda Vayasa describes rightly in this verse the purposes for which God sends Prophets and Gurus, but the words 'I am born in every age' do go against the fundamental nature of God, which has even been stressed in several other verses of Bhagavad Geeta itself. These words bring in the phenomenon of 'Incarnation of God' implying births and deaths of God in different bodies. If the purposes for which God sends True Teachers include establishment of goodness and destruction of wickedness, the Teachers have to preach to the peoples of the world the existence of God and His excellent attributes, because He is the source of all goodness, by remembering whom human beings also acquire qualities of goodness. For destruction of the wicked and wickedness, the Teachers have also to guide human beings to shun the source of evil which is Haumai, the sense of I-ness and Self-pride, but

1. Chinmayananda, Swami, (tr. by), *Bhagavad Geeta*, Chapter IV-8, p. 85.

the words 'I am Incarnation of God' are high sounding words exhibiting not 'Truth' but 'Self-pride' and they can stand in the way of the very purpose which the True Teachers are ordained to perform in the world.

Like Lord Krishna who preached through his sermon recorded in the Bhagavad Geeta, the existence of the Eternal and Immortal God and His excellent attributes, similarly the Prophets of Christianity and Islam, Jesus Christ and Muhammad, also preached the existence and qualities of One Eternal and Immortal God, and their teachings are recorded in the Holy Bible and Holy Quran. However in the case of the latter Holy books also the recordings were made not by the Prophets themselves but by others many decades after the death of the Prohets. It is evident that these Prophets also carried the message of God and wanted to preach worship of God, His greatness and His praises. But if the words used by Vyasa, resulted in the epithet of 'Incarnation of God' in the case of Lord Krishna, in the case of these Prophets the words used were the 'Only son of God' and 'Last Messenger of God'. The writers of Holy Bible, Matthews, Mark, Luke and John, as also the writers of Holy Koran, in the subsequent period of the third Caliph Othman from the records available from Khateebs kept on pieces of palm leaves, stone or other such material, may have used these words for reasons of their own, in the circumstances then prevalent but no rational mind can understand that in the infinite time that passed before Jesus Christ's advent, God never had any Son[1], nor He will have one in the

1. *Note* : God is Father and all human beings are His sons. In this sense all True Teachers describe God as Father and so has done Jesus Christ himself. But if someone depicts Christ as the only begotten son of God, this means falsifying the True Nature of God and lowering Him to the nature of man. Even when everyone is free to have his faith as he likes, so far as the philosophy of Guru Nanak is concerned God is running the world by a Law which is the same for all human beings. He Himself is formless spiritual power and remains above this Law governing human beings. The Guru says "By His Will, God, the Lord of Highest Will, has established a Law for all; He is watching the working of this Law with interest, Himself remaining above such a Law". (Hukmi Hukam chalaae raah; Nanak vigsai veparvah (Nanak-I—Japji). Earlier the Prophet of Islam also

infinite future and also after Prophet Muhammad no other Prophet of God will come to the world, in the infinite time in future. These words on the other hand are conducive to shift the ideas about God's greatness to ideas about greatness of these Prophets themselves. The consequence is visible already and compaigns of religious conversions by these Semitic religions, even by use of force, are based mainly on the ideas of superiority and greatness of the Prophets, because God is the same for all. This situation has created amongst people of Semitic religions a sense of self aggrandisement and Self-pride which increases evil and wickedness in the world, thus standing in the way of the work which True Teachers were required to perform. If it is held that the Prophets have come to reveal the message about God and the Holy books embody such revelations, then the Prophets who carries the revelation cannot be treated higher than Him whom he has come to reveal. Neither can a Messenger be treated higher than Him whose message he carries. An agent cannot be higher than his Master. In this case Master is One but agents can be many. If each Agent is made to claim 'I am unique', 'I am the Only' then this can lead to and is actually leading to higher devotion to the personalities of the Agents instead of to God, who is really 'the Only', 'the Unique' and common to all.

In the case of Guru Nanak all his teachings are recorded in the Adi Granth in original in his own words[1]. His words are

had referred to, in the Holy Koran, about this incidence of the birth of Christ, indicating that in whatever way Christ's birth from a virgin mother may have taken place by the Will of God, he cannot be described as a begotten son of God. The Holy Koran records "Those who say 'the Lord of Mercy has begotten a son' preach a monstrous falsehood, at which the very heavens might crack, the earth break asunder, and the mountains crumble to dust. That they should ascribe a son to the Merciful, when it does not become Him to beget one".

(Dawood, N. J., (tr.), *The Koran*, 19-88, p. 37).

1. *Note*: About these original records, the English author M.A. Macauliffe says "The Sikh religion differs as regards the authenticity of the dogmas, from most other great theological systems. Many of the great Teachers, the world has known, have not left a line of their own compositions, and we only know what they taught through tradition, or second hand information. If Pythagoras wrote any or his tenets, his

in the form of spiritual poetry which cannot be altered, but they give clear guidance on all the fundamental aspects of human life. He was a born Teacher and while a small boy he was sent to school. But when the Teacher asked him to repeat and write the alphabetical words, he told the Teacher instead, the meanings of alphabetical words which are recorded in the Adi Granth under the heading 'Patti likhi' meaning 'Wrote the Alphabet'. Again while a boy he was asked to wear 'Yagyo pavit' or 'sacred thread' as was the custom of Hindu religion but he refused and said to the Pandit who was engaged for the ceremony "Make mercy as cotton, contentment as thread, continence as its knot and Truth as its twist; This is the sacred thread of human mind; If you have 0' Pandit, let me also have it."[1] Even being a born Guru he did not claim for himself any extraordinary status such as 'Incarnation of God' etc. which were attached to previous Prophets. On the other hand he used for himself words of great humility such as 'servant of all' (Das), 'servant of servants' (Dasan Das), 'a singer of God's praises' (Dhadi) etc. But he laid the strongest possible stress on the principle that human worship should be directed to One formless God, to whom are due all praises, highest devotion and epithets of greatness. No human being

writings have not descended to us. We know the teachings of Socrates only through the writings of Plato and Xonophon. Buddha has left no written memorials of his teachings. Kung-fu-tze, known to Europeans as Confucious, left no documents, in which he detailed the principles of his moral and social system. The founder of Christianity did not reduce his doctrines to writings and for them we are obliged to trust the gospels according to Mathew, Mark, Luke and John. The Arabian Prophet did not himself reduce to writing the chapters of the Quran. They were written or compiled by his adherents and followers. But the compositions of the Sikh Gurus are preserved, and we know at first hand what they taught. They employed the vehicle of verse, which is generally unalterable by copyists, and we even become, in time, familiar with their styles. No spurious compositions or extraneous dogmas can therefore be represented as theirs". (Macauliffe, M. A., *The Sikh Religion*).

1. Daya kapah, santokh soot, jat gandhi, sat vat;
Ih janeu jea ka, haih ta pande ghat.
(Nanak I—Rag Asa).

who is born and dies should usurp that greatness and uniqueness which is due to God.

Guru Nanak's way of projecting his teachings to the people was also different from that of previous Teachers. Supposing there is a difficult river to be crossed and it is full of dangerous pit falls and rocks below the water surface. Anyone who is well aware of such pitfalls and rocks can guide others to cross the river in two ways. One is that he stands on a high place on the bank and goes on giving directions to people who are crossing, 'turn this way', 'turn that way' 'go right' 'go left' etc. The other way is that he joins the people and guides them to go along with himself on the safe and right path. Guru Nanak adopted the latter way. The previous Prophets by their extraordinary status as 'Incarnation of God' etc. had created between themselves and their followers a great difference and distance while Guru Nanak said 'I am one of you' 'I am your servant' and joins them. Human soul is to cross the vast and difficult ocean of life. This ocean has many pitfalls and impediments like lust, greed, anger, attachment pride etc., which are all different forms of 'Haumai'. If the human soul is caught up in these impediments of 'Haumai' it remains in the cycle of births and deaths. Only if it can avoid the impediments of Haumai it can reach the other side which means Liberation from life and rejoining God-Soul. Guru Nanak says "This soul is caught up in Haumai; But if Haumai is overcome and eliminated then this 'I' will not fall in the cycle of births and deaths".[1] Again the Guru says "We are fools, our minds are devoid of right sense; We perform our actions with the evil sense of Haumai; This evil is avoided by the kind guidance of a True Guru, Then God showers His blessings and lifts us unto Himself".[2] We observe that in the above verses the Guru uses the word 'I' and 'We' in stressing the need to shun Haumai. This is so because he has joined the crowd of ordinary people whom he wants to cross the ocean of life success-

1. Honda phariag Nanak jaan; Na Hau na mai juni paan.
(Nanak I—G.G.S., p. 1289).
2. Ham moorakh moorakh man mahi; Haumai vich sab kaar kamahi;
Gur parsadi Haumai jaae; Aape bakhse laya milaae.
(Nanak III—G.G.S., p 666).

fully. He associates himself with people who are caught in the evil of Haumai and in great humility uses the words 'I' and 'We' and also says on behalf of all 'We are fools'. At another place in Adi Granth the Guru says "Those who are treated lower than the lowest (by caste or worldly riches), Nanak is a companion to them; Having nothing to do with the high caste and the rich; where lowly and poor are cared for, there are Thy blessings O' Merciful God".[1] In numerous verses of this nature in the Adi Granth the Sikh Gurus have presented a picture of great humility and complete absence of self-pride and self-aggrandisement. In fact to be effective in removing the self-pride and Haumai of their followers, the Teachers themselves, not only have to be free from Self-pride but also appear to be so. Otherwise the people are ever ready to catch at anything that can boost up their sense of superiority over others, and they take advantage of the high sounding and unique epithets of their Teachers.

The tragedy of this situation is that the institution of True Teachers having the most noble objective of spreading the greatness of God and His worship in the world, becomes a veritable impediment in the way of that objective, creating instead divisions, enmities and conflicts amongst peoples who attach all importance and greatness to their respective Teachers, instead of to the common God of all.

1. Neechan ander neech jaat, neechi hu at neech;
Nanak tin ke sang saath, vadian sio kia rees;
Jithai neech samalian, tithai nadar teri bakhsheesh.
(Nanak I, G.G.S., p. 15).

16

TRUE TEACHER

Guide not God

If in the case of some religions, the highest devotion which is due to God has shifted, to a great extent, to the Avtars and Prophets, there are some other religions which have eliminated God altogether from their systems. As we observed, from the earliest times, knowledge about which has come to us, great endeavours have been made by sincere minds, sages, Rishis, Saints, Avtars, Prophets and Gurus, to find out and project to the world the Truth and Reality about the universe. It has been found that this universe, with all its planets, stars, suns, moons, glaxies etc. is functioning within the bounds of a precise and intelligent Law, Method or Order. The solar and lunar eclipses and other cosmic phenomena, are occuring within such a Law at precise times mostly calculable by human beings. A conclusion has been arrived at by an overwhelmingly large intelligent view, that there is a Supreme Intelligent Power, which is the Creator of this universe and is behind all its wonderful functioning. It has been found that this Supreme Power is omnipresent, omnipotent, omniscient, Immortal and Eternal but invisible and formless. Guru Nanak has further held that human soul is eternal as a part of the Supreme Soul but it has a conscious part of I-ness or Haumai, which is not eternal but is carried by the eternal soul in different bodies in the cycle of births and deaths. Great investigations have also been carried out by scientists of parapsychology, to understand the travel of soul from one body to another. Even when it is not a general rule, in thousands of cases, it has been found that some souls remember their past events which they experienced as I-nesses of their previous bodies. This proves, as all scientific truths are proved, firstly that human soul is immortal and does not die with its body and secondly it has a part of I-ness or Haumai which moves along with the soul in different bodies and remembers and explains its experiences of previous lives. If the movement of an invisible soul from one body to another is proved to be a Reality, it is perfectly logical to assume that the invisible Supreme soul of God, which controls such movements of human souls, under a just and regular Law, is also a Truth and Reality.

Budhism and Jainism have eliminated God from their systems, but both do not deny the phenomenon of transmigration of souls, as well as the Law of Karma by which good or bad actions fetch corresponding rewards. One of the good actions, for instance, which is believed by both is 'Ahimsa' meaning non-injury and non-killing of other jivas. But if some one commits the bad action of killing another person, in such a case who arranges the corresponding reward these religions do not explain. Also if Budhism says that human soul is not permanent and dies with the death of body, who suffers the reward of killing and what is the sense in the belief in Transmigration of soul, are matters left unexplained. Surely a murderer cant pass orders for punishment of himself as a reward of his evil act. The irrational teachings of these religions, opposed to one of the most important Truth to which the world has arrived at are self-evident. To eliminate from their systems the source of all goodness, truth and bliss and then to expect that truth, virtue and happiness will prevail in the world instead of 'Asatya' and 'Dukha' by the teachings of these religions is to expect an impossibility. Falsehood and sufferings are increasing in the world and these religions, and in fact all others who do not carry right faith in the existence of God, are adding their substantial contributions to this result. If one main function for which True Teachers come to the world is to preach existence of God and His excellent qualities and the Teachers of these religions, have put themselves in place of God to be worshipped, their systems are bound to go the way of Lokyatika, which increased evil before it was extinct. No structure of morality can stand without the foundation of the Truth of Spirituality.

Like Guru Nanak all his successor Gurus, in their very large number of poetical compositions, embodied in the Adi Granth, express their intense love and devotion to the One Real God, using for themselves, words of great humility. Another significant fact is that all of them call themselves Nanak indicating that their spirit is not different from that of Guru Nanak. This is a rare divine phenomenon. Guru Angad, the second Guru was a petty shopkeeper in a village Khandur of Punjab. The third Guru, Amar Das, was also one among the ordinary citizens of those times, just a trader of a small town Basarke, and so were the other successor Gurus, but as soon as they assumed the Guruship, they were able to compose poetry of a high spiritual order, all calling themselves Nanak, and these compositions were embodied in the Adi Granth. This was so because they received the enlightened spirit of Guru Nanak and Guru Nanak himself received that enlightenment from God Almighty whom he described as his Guru. He says "Nanak has been blessed by his Guru, who is Supreme Almighty God Himself."[1] All the Sikh Gurus, as True Teachers, made a tremendous effort to lead mankind towards the One common God of all, and also to save them from the evil force of Haumai, Self-pride and Selfishness, both by precept and example. But no one claimed 'I am the truest Teacher' or 'I am the Only' through whom human beings can rise upto God and achieve liberation. Rather they had all respect for previous Teachers, who also wanted to raise human beings towards God. Their prayer to God as recorded in the Adi Granth is "O God, Show Thy Mercy and save the world, which is burning in agony; Raise human beings unto Thyself, no matter from which door Ye do so."[2] All True Teachers are different

1. Ampramper parbrahm Parmesar, Nanak Gur milia soe jio.
(Nanak I—G.G.S., p. 599).

2. Jagat jalanda rakh lai apni kirpa dhar;
Jit duarai ubhrai titai lio ubhar. (Nanak III—G.G.S., p. 853).

doors when the destination is the same One God. This was not mere prayer but was proved by practice when, while compiling the volume of the Adi Granth, the fifth Guru, Arjan Dev, included therein the spiritual compositions of so many Saints of God professing other religions. The only criterion was that they treated God as the object of highest devotion and worship instead of the Teachers (doors) through whom they rose higher on the spiritual ascent. Thus this sacred volume gives a place of honour to the hymns of Hindu Saints, Nam Dev, Kabir, Jai Dev, Ravi Das and others and of Muslim Saints Farid and Bhikhan. Jai Dev was a Brahmin but Nam Dev, Kabir and Ravi Das were treated by Hindus as Sudras or low caste. However for the Sikh Gurus what mattered was their highest love of God and absence of any self-pride in them. In fact the Guru rejected inclusion of spiritual sayings of some other Saints which did not fulfil this criterion and exhibited Self-pride.

Guru Gobind Singh the tenth and last living embodiment of the divine spirit of Guru Nanak, in fulfilment of the great task commenced by Guru Nanak issued a stern warning against treating Teachers, the Gurus, as Incarnations of God, "Those who call us Incarnations of God are treading their way straight to the dark dungeon of hell."[1] From this warning by Guru Gobind Singh and numerous verses of Guru Granth Sahib and above all the fundamental principles enunciated in Guru Nanak's Mool Mantar it is abundantly clear that the word 'Guru' or 'Satguru' when implying the personality of a True Teacher is not to be equated to God. However a True Teacher deserves to be fully respected, shown full reverence and obedience, and offered all possible service. The Sikh Gurus have treated their predecessor Gurus in this way and done exceedingly sincere service to them but taking them not as God Himself but as means to show them the way to God.

There are, of course, certain verses in Guru Granth Sahib which indicate that Guru has become God and Guru and God are not different but the same. In all such cases it is necessary to understand the real implication thereof. The Guru's job,

1. Jo ham ko parmesar uchar hain; Te sab narak kund meh par hain. .
(Nanak X—Bachitar Natak-32).

as mentioned earlier, is to raise human soul to become like God-soul and ultimately to rejoin the latter. This becomes possible when the I-consciousness or 'Haumai', attached to human soul, is completely subdued so that all human actions become according to the Will of God—Consciousness in man. In such a case the inner I-consciousness and God-consciousness become virtually the same and man becomes a 'Jivan—Mukta' or 'Liberated while still in life'. In this sense the True Teachers and God are described the same but this implies rising up of man-soul to become God-like, not God coming down to become man-like.[1] Guru Nanak's soul having been sent to the world by God with His own blessings was God-like from the beginning yet he never said 'I am God' as a man in a mortal body has limitations while God is above all limitations. The successor Gurus of Guru Nanak were not Gurus from their births but assumed the spirit of Guruship at some stage of

1. *Note*:—It is in this sense, for instance, that the fifth Guru says in Sukhmani 'Brahm Gyani aap parmeshar'. Brahm Gyani is envisaged here as a living human being with a body, but at the stage of Jivan-Mukta. Brahm Gyan or knowledge of God is achieved by a conscious soul not by any material part of a body. The meaning of this verse is 'Human soul which achieves knowledge of God becomes like Supreme Soul of God Himself'. Similarly 'Brahm Gyani sab srisht ka karta' means 'Human Soul which achieves knowledge of God becomes like Supreme Soul of God, the Creator of universe'. Brahm Gyani's and Jivan Muktas, as living beings with human bodies can be many individuals. If each of such individuals is equated to God, there will be as many Gods and Creators of universe. Thus no one in a body can be equated to God and the above verses should be interpretted accordingly. The Guru has also said about Brahm Gyani 'Man (Mind) apne hai sab te neecha' and 'Brahm Gyani te kachh bura na bhia' meaning that the Soul of Brahm Gyani treats itself not with pride but lower than others and it does not commit any wrong action. Thus the meaning of any particular verse have to be understood, keeping in view other verses of the whole Adi Granth. In fact the teachings of the Sikh Gurus embodied in the Adi Granth are in the form of spiritual poetry full of intense love and longing for God, as well as a strong urge for human beings to rise towards God. These contents are not in the form of ready made principles of philosophy. The latter are to be understood and formulated from the whole, in the same way as the philosophical systems, the Darsanas, or Hindu Shastras, have been understood and formulated from the entire Vedic literature and the Upanisads.

their lives when their souls were raised up, to become God-like.

A number of Hindu scholars who were Brahmans settled in eastern Punjab on the bank of a small river had been touring all round in northern Bharat meeting holy men and Hindu Pandits of high name and fame, discussing spiritual matters. During some of such tours they happened to meet Sikh Gurus as well. Once they came rather in a large group, to meet the fifth Guru, Arjan Dev, while he was at Goindwal, a beautiful town on a plateau on the bank of river Beas. Here Sikhs in their hundreds gathered daily in congregations to hear the divine preachings of the Guru. These Brahmin scholars were so much impressed by the personality and preachings of the Guru that according to their own words, they had found the right place for spiritual solace and uplift, after wandering in vain for years. Their own declaration that it was their good fortune which brought them to the Guru, shows that they were seekers of Truth, not mere 'Bhatts' as they were called. This was a parallel experience of theirs, to that of the Aryans who had first arrived at this very part of Bharat, the land of five rivers, about three thousand years back and had declared that they had found their destination after wading through so many countries. These Brahmin scholars acquired here the knowledge about the works of the five Gurus from Guru Nanak to Guru Arjan Dev. Finding the Gurus with sublime spirituality yet steeped in great humility and love for even the lowest of human beings, their scholarship and inner longing for Reality burst into praise of the work of all the five Gurus, as had been the case of Aryans whose wonder of cosmic entities had burst into what later on formed the Ved-mantras. These Brahmins felt their inner selves raised to a high spiritual plane, also realising the divine heights to which the five Gurus had reached. This spiritual poetry of theirs was of the nature of practical demonstration of theoretical theories how human souls rise up, to get near God-Soul and ultimately to become like the latter, just as scientific theories are followed by practical demonstrations, to prove scientific truths. Guru Arjan Dev therefore gave this poetry of the Bhatts a place in Guru Granth Sahib, so that people may understand the process of soul uplift. For instance for the rise of the soul of Guru Amar Das, Brahmin poet Bhikha says "Guru Amar Das has subdued the sense of lust anger etc. his mind is in perfect peace, his soul is living in God-consciousness, he has understood the Will of God and achieved His knowledge; In this age of Kalyug his soul has become like the soul of God, the Creator of unverse; God knows how this stage of sameness is brought about by Him; Says Bhikha, I have met and seen Guru Amar Das in that exalted stage of peace and bliss."[1] In this way even when I-consciousness and God-consciousness in man become virtually the same and God and Guru are described as the same, in accordance with the philosophy of Guru Nanak, the Guru does not become entitled to claim 'I am God' or 'I am Incarnation of God'. A Guru, True Teacher, Avtar or Prophet, while in a material body has to say 'he is my father', 'she is my mother', 'I was born in that year', 'I have to die some day' etc. and all these constitute limitations which do not apply to God. If some one in a body says 'I am God' he brings in, one form of God, somebody else could also say 'I am God' and he will bring in another form of God and so on the process can continue. This results in giving a turn to the worship of One to worship of many. Guru Nanak who came to be called 'Nanak Nirankari' because he preached formless God, strongly stressed two main points. Firstly to worship God through His name not through any form, calling such worship as 'Naam japna' and secondly not allowing the sense of Haumai to stand in the way between human beings and God by claiming for the True Teachers 'My Teacher is God Himself' 'My Teacher is the greatest', 'Mine is the Only' 'Mine is the Last none to come after him' and so on, as all these claims of superiority are causing divisions and conflicts in mankind. Let fundamental nature of God remain intact and same for all. Amongst the Sikhs a tradition has come to be accepted 'Worship only Immortal God; Get guidance of

1. Kaam karodh vas karai, pavan udant na dhavai;
Nirankar kai vasai des, Hukam bujh veechar paavai;
Kal mai roop karta purakh, so jaanai jin kichh keeho;
Gur milio soe, Bhikha kahai, sehj rang darsan deeo.
(Swayye Mohale teeje ke 3—G.G.S., p. 1395).

Guru's words; See God in Khalsa; Do good to all human beings."[1] Guru's words constitute real Guru which give guidance to man. Guru Nanak while having a discussion with some holy men who asked him several questions said in reply to one "The real Guru means the words of guidance uttered by him; and real disciple is the human mind which grasps and acts upon such words."[2]

Ultimately a time arrived when another most significant step was taken so that all mankind may realise the presence of the all pervading formless God and offer their highest devotion direct to him. By the hard and sincere work of all the ten Gurus, involving great sacrifices on their parts, the infrastructure with all its necessary parts, had been created both for God-worship (Bhagti) as well as for the sense of strength (Shakti) in man, necessary to meet challenges of the world. The sacred volume of the Adi Granth had been completed by Guru Gobind Singh by adding therein the spiritual compositions of the ninth Guru, Tegh Bahadur. If Guru Nanak had said that Real Guru meant the words of guidance spoken by the Gurus, Guru Gobind Singh, now realising the arrival of the end of his physical life, declared in a congregation, called for the purpose, that Guru Granth Sahib, will be the future everlasting Guru of the Sikhs, thus removing even the intermediary physical personalities of the Teachers. Guru Granth Sahib is altogether free from Self-pride and selfishness as it does not ask and covet any worldly things, but it is the custodian of the spirit of the Gurus and contains all the guidance required by human beings to achieve the objective of their lives. This sacred volume fulfils eminently the role of a True Teacher. It does not contain any historical and mythological stories, any rituals, any superstitions etc. and in fact it contains nothing which could be called sectarian. Its guidance is applicable to humanity as a whole. It constitutes a synthesis of the common fundamental

1. 'Puja Akal Ki; Parcha Gur shabad ka;
Deedar Khalse ka; Bhalla sarbat ka lochna".
2. Shabad Guru Surat dhun chela.
(Nanak I—Sidh Gost, G.G.S., p. 943).

values projected by all religions as the Sikh Gurus are sitting herein in spirit along with the spirits of saints of both oriental and semitic theistic religions in a bond of love and affection amongst each other and highest devotion to One common God of all. It can bring about love and brotherhood amongst all people and guide them to achieve objective of their human lives.

17

THE REAL DHARMA

In a previous chapter we observed a Truth which was earlier divulged in Bhagavad Geeta that whenever there is decline of Dharma in our world, God sends a True Teacher to reinstate Dharma. Here we have to understand what is the true implication of the word 'Dharma'. When advent of Guru Nanak took place in the fifteenth century he also observed a great decline of Dharma and said "The age has taken the shape of a butchers knife, the rulers themselves have become butchers; Dharma has taken wings and vanished; There is darkness of falsehood everywhere and light of Truth and righteousness is nowhere visible."[1] In the seventeenth century Guru Gobind Singh declared "Well understand, all ye men of God; the purpose for which I have taken birth here in this world; It is to establish Dharma, to uplift men of God and uproot the forces of evil."[2]

The word Dharma is used variously but its literal meanings are generally taken as 'Essential and righteous Duty'. Guru Nanak and his successor Gurus have amply clarified in

1. Kal Kaati, Raje kasai Dharam pankh kar udria;
Koor amavas sach chandrma deesai naahi kai chariha.
(Nanak I—G.G.S., p. 145).
2. Yehi kaaj dhara ham janmag;
Samjh lio sadhu sab manmang;
Dharam chalavan, Sant ubharan Dusht sabon ko mool uparan.
(Nanak X—Bachiter Natak).

their spiritual compositions the correct implication of Dharma. But all along these past centuries and during these present times this word Dharma is being grossly misunderstood and is usually equated to Religion, which means an organised institution more appropriately represented by Indian words Panth, Matt, Sampardaya etc. In stanza N. 34 of Japji Guru Nanak says "In the midst of the setting of nature, with its days and nights, weathers, air, water,fire and its lower regions, God has kept the planet Earth, as a place where all human being may practice Dharma."[1] Again he says in Japji "O God the air, water, fire, the bounties given by Thee are all singing Thy praises, so is Dharam Raj, the power created by Thee to watch practice of Dharma by human beings; Thy conscious power and invisible power (Chit-Gupt) existing in each human being to write down continuously the practice of Dharma by each, is also singing Thy praises."[2] Evidently the word Dharma is used by Guru Nanak in a sense that it is something which is expected to be practiced by each and every human being who is born here on this earth.

But what is that Dharma which is essential for each and every human being? In fact it is necessary to know what for a human being has taken birth ? Is it for eating and drinking, nourishing up the physical body, doing all sorts of vocational works to meet the needs of the body growth, working hard during day, resting at night and then die one day ? This is evidently not the purpose of human life, because this much is essential even for animals. A human being is also an animal but a spiritual one, and it has been bestowed upon by Nature the highest thinking power as compared to all other animals. It must, therefore, excercise that thinking power to understand who has sent him to this world and for what purpose. As indicated ealier uncoun-

1. Rati Ruti Thiti Var; Pawan paani, agni, patal;
Tis vich dharti thaap rakhi Dharamsal.
(Nanak I—Japji).
2. Gaveh tuhnu paun paani baisantar; Gaveh raja Dharam Dware;
Gaveh Chit-Gupt likh jaaneh; Likh likh Dharam Veechare.
(Nanak I—Japji).

ted human beings have actually excercised their thinking power on this problem and have come to certain conclusions. Guru Nanak has said 'No one takes birth by his own will; Neither is death within one's own will."[1] He has also said that God is the Creator of the universe including human beings as well as of all bounties of life necessary for their sustenance. It is therefore the essential duty of each and every human being to be grateful to its creator for giving it the opportunity of human life and also providing all essential things for sustenance of this life. The way to express such gratitude, according to Guru Nanak, is to worship God through remembrance of His Name. God being source of all goodness such remembrance of His Name will create qualities of goodness in the worshipper, who will be performing virtuous deeds in the world. Such good deeds will take the worshipper nearer to God and ultimately enable his soul to rejoin Him. Guru Nanak has said "The good and bad deeds performed by human beings are being watched by God's Power of judging Dharma of man; By one's own good or bad deeds some get near to Him and others get away from Him; Those who have worshipped Him by meditation on His Name have accomplished the hard task for which they have come to the world; O' Nanak they get honour in the divine Court and liberate numerous others along with themselves."[2]

Thus it is indicated that the two main items which constitute universal 'Dharma of man', according to Guru Nanak are, firstly remembrance of God's Name and secondly performance of good deeds. What type of deeds can be treated as good and universally applicable to every human being are amply clarified in Guru Granth Sahib, as already indicated in the previous chapter. But the two main items constituting the Essential Duty of each and every human being or

1. Jor na jiwan maran na jor. (Nanak I—Japji).
2. Changiaaia buriaaia wachai Dharam Hadur;
Karmi aapo aapni ke nere ke door,
Jini Naam dhiaaia gaya maskat ghaal;
Nanak te mukh ujle keti chhuti naal. (Nanak I—Japji).

'Dharma of man' are further clarified by the Guru who says "The highest Dharma out of all that is treated as Dharma is Remembrance of God's Name and performance of good deeds."[1]

The English word Religion is derived from two Latin words 're' and 'legere' which together mean 'to bind back' and thus Religion is an organised institution which binds human beings in a number of beliefs and disciplines. Taking a pragmatic view of the various world religions, as they actually exist, we observe that a Religion includes mainly the following five types of beliefs. Firstly belief in a Supreme Power higher than that of a human being itself whether He is called God or given any other name. Secondly belief in a Prophet, Avtar or Guru and in the holy scriptural books associated with them. Thirdly belief in the path proper or method prescribed by the spiritual Teachers and included in their scriptural or subsidiary books, for achieving the objective of human life, as for instance Path of virtuous actions (Karam marg), or understanding the Reality of the Supreme Power (Gyan marg), or Devotional worship of a deity or deities (Bhakti marg). Fourthly belief in Mythology assisting to understand the basic principles of each religion and in cosmology, cosmogony and eschatology, by which are governed the lives and deaths of human beings according to those religions. Fifthly beliefs in various rituals, ceremonials, rules of discipline applicable to each religion.

All such beliefs cover a very vast ground and on all these important five aspects different world religions have their own beliefs propounded by their own Prophets. As however those Prophets have been coming to the world at different times and at different places and when different circumstances were prevalent, all these numerous beliefs could not be the same and have not actually been the same in so many respects. But because they come to be included in the holy books associated with different Teachers they became integral part of each religion. People following different religions felt bound by

1. Sarb Dharam mai saresht Dharam;
Har ko Naam jap nirmal karam. (Nanak V—Sukhmani).

all those beliefs included in their holy books which were considered by some religions as revelations from God Himself. This created a situation that people of our world became divided in religious groups each having so many different beliefs besides a few common ones. As the former different beliefs were numerous they dominated and various religions became opposing forces and in some cases enimical to each other, obscuring and relegating to a backward position the few common beliefs.

To Guru Nanak this situation appeared to be altogether un-natural and unsatisfactory. He said even if each religion is one whole, it has two distinct parts. One is the Essence part and the other is the ways and means part, or the Methodology, which is just to assist or help in achieving the Essence. The Essence part of all world religions is substantially similar. Considering the case of theistic religions all of them have the common belief that God is One. All of them also have similar beliefs about the fundamental attributes of God that He is omnipotent, omnipresent, omniscient etc. There is also substantial similarity about the belief that human beings come from God and have ultimately to revert to Him on achievement of 'Mukti', 'Liberation' 'Nijat' etc. To achieve such ultimate stage the practice of high spiritual and moral values during the course of worldly life also have much in common. That each individual requires the guidance of a True Teacher in order to reach that ultimate stage of Liberation, is also a common belief.

All these common parts of all theistic religions tend to raise human beings towards God and constitute the Essence part of these religions. In so far as they create an urge in human beings to worship One common God they create in them the virtuous qualities of which God is the source and which are essential for all human beings. Thus common parts can also be called the Dharma part of each such religion. So far as the Sikh religion is concerned Guru Nanak and his successor gurus have separated its Dharma and Methodology parts. Dharma part, which is universally applicable to all human beings, is included in the Adi Granth which has been given the status of Guru Granth Sahib by the tenth Guru,

Gobind Singh. Guru Gobind Singh also arranged that Methodology part of Sikh religion or the Khalsa Panth, be enshrined in separate codes called 'Rehtnamas', containing the organisational rules and disciplines. Guru Granth Sahib, as already indicated, does not embody such organisational rules and disciplines. Neither does it contain any historical narratives, mythology, rituals, superstitions etc. The intention of the Gurus evidently was that Guru Granth Sahib be a magna charta of universal Dharma of man. Dharma is the most important part of a religion and no one can achieve objective of human life without practicing such Dharma. Whereas the objective of life of a human being is rising towards God and ultimately rejoining Him, the objective of a True Teacher is to guide human beings to achieve their objective. Thus the objectives of human beings and their True Teachers are complimentary to each other. For this purpose the Teacher does create an organised circle of his own in order that human beings may continue to get his guidance and therefore he prescribes certain organisational rules and disciplines for his own circle. Each such circle constitutes a religion which has two parts as already indicated above.

But what needs to be understood clearly is that Dharma part must be treated as of higher importance than the Methodology part. To Dharma therefore must be attached highest priority even though the Methodology part of any particular religion may also be essential for those who profess that religion. But treating organisational rules and tenets of greater importance than Dharma part of their religions is definitely a case of assigning wrong priority. However, as we have seen earlier, in Hindu religion, as it is being understood, there is hardly any distinction between its Essence part and its other secondary part. The Vedas as a whole are treated as words of God and all that is included therein is treated as of equal importance. Rather according to Brahmana part of the Vedas constituting the Purva Mimansa philosophy, prescribing sacrifices of animals to deities (Yajnas), burning of incense clarified butter etc. in fire (Homa), giving charities (Dana) and all such karmas (actions) to be performed physically are treated as Dharma of man, even though this philosophy does not concern itself with God at all. Similarly the principle of caste distinctions by which some human beings are treated as having highest privileges, others having medium and yet others having lowest privileges, is treated as Dharma and is called 'Varna Dharma'. This principle gets its original sanction from Sanhita part of the Vedas, as Mantra No. 10-90 of Rig Veda equates symbolically the Brahman to head, the highest part of the body, the Kashatrias and Vaishyas to the medium parts, the arms and legs, and Sudras to feet, the lowest part of the body. The essential and righteous duty or Dharma of Sudras is taken as duty of menials or service of others and they do not have the privilege of hearing and reading the Vedas as if they do not require Mukti as other human beings do, in this precious human life. However Hindu religion also has, as indicated earlier, its Essence part constituted mainly by the Upanisadic part of the Vedas, dealing with worship of One common formless God. It is most essential for those professing this ancient religion, to distinguish between the two parts of their religion and give highest priority to the Real Dharma part.

Similarly the Semitic religions such as Islam and Christianity do have a definite Essence part stressing the existence and greatness of God, treating Him as the highest object of human worship, and doing good deeds of which God is the source. But in their case also such Essence part lies included in their Holy books alongwith the other secondary part. The contents of the Holy Quran and the Holy Bible are treated as revelations from God and therefore of highest importance. If in the case of Vedas for instance, Mantra XII-4-38 of Atharva Veda forbids cooking and eating cow's flesh, Sura 2-173 of Holy Quran borbids eating of flesh of swine. Both these tenets can not be of universal application as essential and righteous duty of all human beings, but they are given so great importance that in communal riots, which have been occurring all along these past centuries after birth of Islam, hundreds of human beings are being killed in the process for upholding the sanctity of these tenets and no sin is deemed to be involved in such killings. It is most essential here also that the Real-Dharma part should be treated higher than the Methodology part. As we observed earlier, both in Christianity and Islam. even when their Prophets had the objective of spreading in the world worship of God and they preached such worship, it is evident that devotion to the Prophets themselves is generally higher than to God.[1] The Christian tenet in Gospel 3-36 "He who believes in the Son has eternal life; He who does not obey the Son shall not see life, but the wrath of God rests upon him", cannot also be of universal application and Essence part of religion, because human beings who worship God with highest devotion, but through other True Teachers, do not earn wrath of God.

The atheist religions of Budhism and Jainism have also their elaborate rules of discipline as well as of morality, and all of these are treated as norms of Dharma. The general laws of morality such as Truthfulness, Right thinking, right action, non-staling etc. are, no doubt, of the nature of universal Dharma applicable to all human beings. These were in fact preached by Buddha as norms which should benefit all human beings in their day to day practical lives. They were as a strong reaction of Buddha against the concept of Dharma prevalent at

1. *Note* : In Islam as between God and Prophet who is offered higher devotion is illustrated by cases such as that of a saint of God, Hazrat Sarmad. We quote a Muslim author, Pir Syed Muhamad Ahmad, who says "When he (Sarmad) read 'Kalma' he used to say 'La Allah' (God is great) but did not say anything further. The knowledge of this fact spread among the general public. When he (Sarmad) was asked why he did not say further (Muhamad Rasool Allah—Muhamad is Prophet of God) he used to reply 'I get so much absorbed in devotion to God that my aim becomes to realize God first. I could proceed further only thereafter". But for such devotion to God and not to Prophet, the Muslim Kazi of empror Aurangzeb adjudged Sarmad as deserving the punishment of death and Sarmad was executed by the orders of Aurangzeb. The grave of Sarmad stands near the famous Jama Masjid of Delhi. It is clear that Sarmad being a Muslim had faith both in God and in Prophet Muhamad, but had higher love and devotion to God than to his Prophet and for this main fault on his part, he had to lose his life, even though he was also charged for breaking some other rules of 'Shariat' the Muslim rules of discipline, such as not wearing clothes as required by those rules.

that time under Vedic philosophy of rituals, involving sacrifices of animals in Yajnas, burning of incences ghee etc. in Homa and other karmkandas which were not concerned with day to day moral behaviour amongst human beings but were believed to bring their rewards after death in the life of Heaven (Swarga). Buddha did not agree that the Vedic provisions had any divine authority and treated the provisions of future rewards of Brahmanical rituals as empty promises. Thus norm of morality preached by Buddha certainly had a greater value as universal Dharma than the Brahmnical ritual, which he wanted to discard, but the pity was that Buddha threw away the baby along with the bath water. With the presence of a strong force of Haumai in human minds it is but natural that such morality of Buddha may wither away when it is cut off from its source of God, just as a plant withers away when cut off from its soil.

Guru Nanak also gave to the world an elaborate code of moral virtues but without cutting it from God, the unlimited source of all goodness and virtue. J.J. Karam mentions some of the norms of morality which he discovered in the Adi Granth of Guru Nanak, both the evils to be avoided and virtues to be practiced: "Nanak's teachings cover both the spiritual perspective as well as ethical objectives. He has laid down a rigid ethical Code for the seekers. The catalogue of vices, either to be avoided or eliminated, as impediments to the upward march, is quite big, enumerating among other things, lust, anger, greed, infatuations, ego, avarice, jealousy, enmity, gossip, moral fickleness, double standards; superstitions, ritualism, untruth, loquacity, disputatiousness, intoxicants and indulgences in various other sensual pleasures and desires. The list of virtues that are to be acquired and developed, as aids to the evolutionary process is equally formidable; comprising self-introspection, self-control, self-subdual, self-surrender, dedication, devotion, truth, universal love, compassion, humility, simplicity, contentment and moral discipline (purity of body and mind). In order to be so virtuous the seeker should contemplate on 'Nama' under the guidance of his guru, and in company of saints. Even the worst sinner can be redeemed through reverence, repentence and resolution against the repetition of evil designs and deeds."[1] It is evident that all these norms of morality, both evils to be avoided and virtues to be practiced are of universal application to all human beings and constitute 'Dharma of man'. If Buddhists include in the philosophy of Buddha the principle that soul is not permanent and dies with the body, the soul of Buddha is non-existent for them and the practice of norms of Morality preached by Buddha depend solely on the will of human beings themselves, which by its very nature flows down more readily towards evil than towards virtue. In the case of norms of Morality stressed by Guru Nanak in Guru Granth Sahib, a human being is required to keep the everliving all-pervading spirit of God in his mind-by contemplating on His Name and that sustains and strengthens the moral virtues.

In Guru Granth Sahib two other most important virtues are stressed in various verses such as "One who earns his livelyhood by doing honest vocational work and then consumes his earning only after distribution to the needy, has understood the path of righteousness, says Nanak."[2] These verses make essential for every able-bodied human being performance of some vocational work to sustain and maintain his physical body in a fit condition because this body is custodian of the jivatman which is required to contemplate on the Name of God. To distribute to the disabled, poor and needy out of one's earnings is also within the Essential and Righteous duties of man and these two principles, called 'Dharam-kirt' and 'Wand-Chhakna' form part of Universal Dharma according to Philosophy of Guru Nanak. This Philosophy does not agree with the Jaina philosophy by which great austerities and hardships inflicted on body, keeping it without proper food and

1. Paper in International Seminar, Punjabi University—1969.

Note : For more regarding Morality in this Philosophy, please see Chapter nine "Guru Nanak and Ethics" in this author's book *Nanakism*.

2. Ghal Khaae kichh hathon deh; Nanak rah pachhanai se.
(Nanak IV—Rag Sarang).

clothes, are deemed as meritorious acts of Dharma. If all these norms of morality including the 'Dharam Kirt' and 'Wand-chhakna' as included in Guru Granth Sahib, are understood and practiced as essential and righteous duty of all human beings certainly our world could get relief from much of the divisions, conflicts and sufferings, it is experiencing otherwise. The Sikh Gurus had their own minds steeped in love and longing for God and their words contained in Guru Granth Sahib do have an appeal to human minds to rise towards God and do the noble deeds specified in the sacred volume, and thus have all the potential to change the world conditions for better. In this regard the words of American Noble-prize winner, Miss Pearl S. Buck are relevant, who says "Sri Guru Granth Sahib is a source book, and expression of man's loneliness, his aspirations, his longings, his cry to God and his hunger for communication with that Being. I have studied the scriptures of other great religions, but I don't find elsewhere the same power of appeal to the heart and mind as I find in these volumes They are compact inspite of their length and are revelation of the vast reach of the human heart varying from the most noble conception of God, to the recognition and indeed the insistence upon the practical need of the human body." Thus if austerities of the body, wandering about as recluses and Sanyasis without vocational work, are acts of merit for some religions, in accordance with philosophy of Guru Nanak, proper care of body and doing honest vocational work are included in the Dharma part of the religion.

Much of the misery, sufferings and troubles of the world are due to not distinguishing between the Essence and Methodology parts of religions. Guru Nanak has brought out the concept of two parts of religion and in one of the stanzas (Pauris) of Japji he mentions both 'Panth' and 'Dharma' indicating also which is of higher importance. This is Pauri No. 14 out of the eight Pauris from No. 8 to 15, the four stressing the merits of Hearing the Praise of God and the next four of Believing in God and in 'His Name', representing His real all-pervading spirit. The Guru says "One who reposes firm faith in God does not encounter impediments in his path;

Rather with such firm faith in God he goes his way with honour; With firm faith in God he treads the path of Religion (Panth) also with ease; Because with such faith in God his connection with 'Dharma' gets firmly established."[1] What is of utmost importance is the need for a human being to establish a firm connection with the Dharma part of religion. If that is achieved, treading the path of religion as a whole with its other Methodology part becomes easy. In fact it is more important and also more difficult to avoid lust, anger, greed, falsehood etc. and practice self-control, truth, humility, contentment etc. which constitute Dharma, than to observe the rules and disciplines of the Methodology part of religion.

If in Bhagavad Geeta it is indicated that whenever there is decline of Dharma, God sends some one to reinstate Dharma and if Guru Nanak and Guru Gobind Singh also declared that they have come to the world to reinstate Dharma, surely what is to be reinstated is not the distinction between Brahman and Sudra, what sacrifices are to be offered in Yajnas, what food and flesh should be eaten, or what type of clothes and symbols should be adopted and what other rules of Methodology are to be observed. But what is to be reinstated by Men

1. Manai marag thhak na paae; Manai pat sio pargat jaae;
Manai magan chalai Panth; Mannai Dharam seti sanbandh;
Aisa Naam niranjan hoe; Jeko man jaanai man koe."
(Nanak I—Japji).

Note : Some scholars read the third line of Pauri 14 of Japji as 'Manai mag na chalai Panth" others read it as "Manai magan chalai Panth". The difference is in the word 'Mag na' (two words) and 'magan' (one word). The word 'mag' and 'Panth' both mean Path as 'mag' is a short form of 'marag' and the need of both words in the same line do not make the sense clear. On the other hand with one word 'magan' in line 'magan chalai Panth' this line means 'Treads the path with ease' and this is also consistent with the first two lines of this very stanza which indicate 'meeting no impediments in the path' and this meaning seems more correct. In one of earliest Tikas of Japji by the late Giani Sher Singh the word 'Magan' (one word) is given along with elaborate justification and this is adopted here also.

of God is the Dharma as constituted by worship of One common God of all and practicing the norms of spiritual and Moral values as are explained and elaborated in Guru Granth Sahib. However Guru Nanak has indicated the need to tread the path of religion also. Why is the institution of organised religion also necessary we propose to understand in the next chapter.

18

THE REAL PLACE OF RELIGION

Custodian of Dharma

Dharma is a most precious thing which is needed by every one who is born as a human being, as we observed in the last chapter. But every precious thing needs some suitable device to keep it safe. A precious stone, a diamond, is kept in a fine and strong case. The more precious it is the more security it needs. Milk is a very noursHing food but it requires a vessel for proper preservation before being used. Dharma is the noursHing food for every jivatma but Religion is the vessel to preserve it. But the most vital question remained what steps should be taken that such Dharma may be practiced by all. Guru Nanak had declared in the Slok to Japji that those who worship God by meditation on His Name "get honour in the Divine Court of God and take numerous others along with themselves". The words 'take numerous others along with themselves' indicate another very important and significant principle that it is not sufficient for a human being to practice Dharma and achieve Mukti for himself but he has to take care of the human society also. If a man of Dharma must distribute his earnings to needy and thus care for physical needs of others, he must also care for Spiritual needs of others and this he could do by spreading the concept of Dharma in the world at large.

After creating the concept of 'Dharma of man' with such a unique scope, Guru Nanak planned to create also a 'Man of Dharma' who could practice Dharma himself and also spread it to others. We have to recall the words of Guru Nanak "No Hindu no Musalman' which he declared before proceeding on his first long missionary tour in the year 1498 A.D. At that time he was at Sultanpur in Punjab working as Incharge of the grain store of the Muslim Nawab Daulat Khan Lodhi. Just before leaving that job and proceeding on tour he remained untraceable for three days after entering the river Vaeen for a bath much before dawn as usual. As he said on reappearing, he was given a mission by God Himself which he must fulfil, even when the Nawab, who was happy with his honest work of grain store, and relatives of the Guru himself, entreated him not to leave. At that time Christianity had not come to India and here existed three oriental religions, Hinduism, Jainism and Buddhism besides the Semitic religion of Islam. By mentioning 'No Hindu, no Musalman' what Guru Nanak meant was that before one is called a Hindu, Muslim, Christian, Buddhist, etc. one should at least deserve to be called a 'man' in the real sense of the word. Man should have some qualifications to distinguish him from animals, and these are the qualifications coming within the purview of 'Dharma of man'. However two such qualities are the minimum. Firstly that man should have this much sense at least to say thanks to anyone who does some good to him. God is the creator of man and He has given him all the bounties of life. Man should therefore express his gratefulness to God, by remembering Him. Secondly man should not be so selfish as to live, work, pass his life entirely for himself but he should do also some good to the human society in which he lives. Guru Nanak has therefore stressed most these twin principles of Remembering God and avoiding Selfishness or Haumai.

Guru Nanak was not satisfied with the way in which both Hinduism and Islam were being practiced at that time. The Muslim invaders from the West, ever since the invasion of Sind, the north western province of India, by Muhamad-bin-Qasim in 712 A.D., had been coming frequently and in the name of their religion, been killing and looting the Hindus, pulling down their temples, breaking their idols and dishonouring their women. The Hindus on their side steeped in orthodoxy and ideas of non-violence were unable, in spite of their superior numbers, to resist the tyranny of Muslims. Guru Nanak had witnessed all such killings etc. of Hindus when Mughal Emperor Babur attacked the town of Eminabad in Punjab. The Guru himself was taken prisoner by Babur, though subsequently he was set free when the Invader came to understand that he was a Man of God. By all this situation Guru Nanak realised that 'Man of Dharma' besides 'Bhagti' or Saintliness, essentially required also 'Shakti' or Strength to resist the tyranny and evil in the world. As long as the strong force of Haumai or Selfishness existed in the world, evil and tyranny cannot be ruled out and will continue to exist side by side with goodness. Observing the tyranny of Babur, Guru Nanak had raised his hands in prayer to God Almighty in protest saying "Thou art Lord of all; I would not have protested; If a strong fights a strong; But here a lion is killing cows; Lord Thou hast something more to do here".[1]

Thus for preserving Dharma, with all its values and creating 'Man of Dharma' to spread Dharma in the world at large it was Guru Nanak who originally envisaged formation of a new religious path. For spreading Dharma the 'Man of Dharma' was to be a Saint of God and for resisting evil he was to have the strength of a soldier. His prayer to God to remove imbalance of strength that he saw at the time of Babur's invasion was, in fact, Guru Nanak's resolve to produce a New man, a Saint as well as a soldier. All this meant a great task before Guru Nanak, which could not be accomplished in one life. It was therefore completed in ten lives in all of which the same spirit of Guru Nanak was working. If there was a Spiritual Teacher, Lord Krishna, there was no second Krishna, neither was there a second Christ or a second Muhamad. But in the case of Guru Nanak all the Gurus called themselves Nanak and it was declared in Guru Granth Sahib "The spirit is the same, the method is the same; Only the body is changed".[2] It is not correct to say that Guru Nanak and Guru Gobind Singh had different aims. Guru Gobind Singh

1. Kar a tu sabhna ka soiy; Je sakta, sakte ko maare ta mai ros na hoiy; Sakta sih maare pai vagai, Khasmai sa pursaiy. (Nanak I—Rag Asa).
2. Jot oha jugat saaiy, Seh kaaya bher platiai (G.G.S., p. 966).

said "Many think we are different; But there are others who do realise that we are the same; Those who realise us the same have understood the reality; Others have not".[1] The first five Gurus worked mainly to create 'Bhagti' in the 'Man of Dharma' and produced the magna charta of universal Dharma which was embodied in Guru Granth Sahib. The other five Gurus worked mainly to produce 'Shakti' in the Man of Dharma and to progress further the organisational part of the Panth. Ultimately a time came when the task commenced by Guru Nanak after getting a mission from God Almighty Himself, was completed by Guru Gobind Singh by giving the finishing touches to the structure of new religion and brought out in complete form the Khalsa Panth. If Guru Nanak was originally given a mission by God Himself to commence establishment of a new Panth, Guru Gobind Singh also was given a mission by God Himself while he was worshipping Him at a place called Hemkund in Himalayas in his previous life as he himself has described. That mission was to take birth as a successor of Guru Nanak and complete the job of bringing out the New Panth. He says God ordered him 'I bless you as my son; I assign you the job of bringing out the New Panth; Proceed thou to spread Dharma amongst people pulling them out of the evils of world".[2] Guru Gobind Singh administered 'Amrit', the nectar of life, to the man of Dharma by giving him the symbols both of Saintliness (Bhagti) and Strength (Shakti). The nature has given highest thinking power to man as compared to all other animals and the same nature has given longest hair on man's thinking organ, the head. Spiritual Teachers Rama, Krishna, Christ, Muhamad and others have generally been depicted with long hair and so have been Saints of God professing various religions. That general symbol of spirituality 'the Keshas' was made by Guru Gobind Singh the symbol of Saintliness while a sword (Kirpan) was to

1. Bhin bhin sabhu kar jaana; Ek roop hinhu pehchana;
Jin jana tin hi sidh paaiy; Bin samjhe sidh haath na aaiy.
(Nanak X—Bachitar Natak).

2. "Mai apna sut tohe niwaja; Panth parchur karbe ko saaja; Jaha taha tai Dharam chalae; Kabudh karan te lok hataae;
(Nanak X—Bachitar Natak).

be the symbol of Strength for the new man of his vision. The Kangha (comb) for cleanliness and Kachha (knicker bocker) for continence were also added with the symbol of saintliness while Kara (iron bangle) in hand as a sign from Guru Gobind Singh to use Kirpan only for righteous purposes, was added to the symbol of Strength, thus constituting the five Ks or symbols beginning with the word K. Never before Guru Nanak any spiritual Teacher had envisaged the creation of a man who may be Ideal as one doing honest vocational work as a Saint and as a Soldier at the same time. And never before such a task was completed in a unique manner as was adopted by Guru Gobind Singh who asked sacrifice of heads for the sake of Dharma from those who agreed to become Ideal men of the vision of the Gurus. By such a process Guru Gobind Singh wanted to change the inner thinking, the ideas and vision of man and therefore asked him to repeat fifteen times the declaration "Khalsa is of God; Victory is of God" (Wahiguru ji ka Khalsa; Wahiguru ji ki Fateh). Guru Gobind Singh further said "Khalsa is my own special form; I continue to live in the Khalsa".[1] Guru Gobind Singh himself was a 'Man of God' and he wanted to make the Khalsa like himself in outward appearance as well as in the matter of inner qualities of Dharma. With Amrit and symbols given to him, the Khalsa constituted the front line of the new Panth and he became one step higher as 'Man of God' than the general line of 'Man of Dharma'. But as 'Wahiguru ji ka Khalsa' (man of God) the Khalsa carried the great and heavy responsibility to bring about 'Wahiguru ji ki Fateh' (Victory of God) on earth, instead of the Victory of evil, that of Haumai, Self-pride, and pride such as 'My religion is truest' 'My teacher is Truest' which was prevalent. Such heavy responsibility required the combined force of an organised religion which came into existence as Khalsa Panth. What was to be spread in the world was, of course, the universal Dharma as enshrined in the sacred volume of Guru Granth Sahib.

According to previous thinking which was prevalent in the people, religious convertions of others constituted acts of great

1. Khalsa mero roop hai kha as; Khalse mai hau karon niwas.
(Nanak X—Sarb Loh).

merit. This was so because each religion considered itself superior to others. The Hindus called Muslims 'Malechhas' and Muslims called Hindus as 'Kafirs'. These ideas were based more on the Methodology part of religion than on the Essence part but they created enmities amongst peoples of different religions. The Jews, Christians and Muslims believed in the same One God but they have been fighting with each other as enemies. Such ideas of enmity are continuing even upto these present times due to ignoring the Essence parts of their religions, as historical events in various parts of the world such as Israil, Lebanon, Cyprus, Philipines etc. amply prove. Most of the religious conflicts and wars which have been going on in the world are due to ignoring the higher Dharma part which is present to a substantial extent in all theistic religions. The history of what has been happening to the Sikh Gurus themselves also proves the same.

Guru Arjun Dev, the fifth successor of Guru Nanak, who was so full of love and devotion to God that highest number of hymns, which are embodied in Guru Granth Sahib gushed out from his heart, as songs of deep emotion love and praise of God. He was also the first compiler of the sacred volume containing not only hymns in praise of God of the Sikh Gurus themselves but also of other saints both Hindus and Muslims who were similarly devoted to One God. The Guru was thus preaching worship of God and Universal Dharma as enshrined in the sacred volume but this preaching was not acceptable to the Muslim authority of that time, the Mughal Emperor Jehangir, who was ruling India at that time and who himself says in his autobiography *Tuzk-i-Jehangiri* "On the banks of the river Beas there stands a village Goindwal, where dwells a person, Arjan by name. He is known as Guru. He has taken into his fold quite a number of Hindus and also simple Muhamadans by influence of his ways and manners. His purity and saintliness is being loudly professed on all sides and worshippers from all parts of the country rally around him and pay their homage to him. This movement has been going on for the past three or four generations. I have been contemplating for a long time either to end this movement or convert the Guru to Islam". Having this object in view Jehangir found a small pretext and ordered that the Guru be tortured to death by the Law of Yusa if he refused to be converted to Islam. Jehangir therefore says further 'I was already fully aware of his heresis and as I was now informed of him, I ordered that the Guru be brought into my presence, and I conferred all his belongings to Murtza Hussain Khan, and further ordered that he should be tortured to death under the Law of Yusa."[1] This Law of Yusa meant killing a holy man of God in such a way that shedding of his blood is not involved. The Guru was accordingly tortured by making him sit in a water cauldran under which fire burnt, as it was considered that in this way only blisters will erupt and shedding of blood could be avoided. By boiling water blisters erupted all over the Guru's body. He was then made to sit on a iron sheet heated from below and hot sand was poured all over his blistered body. Yielding to tyranny and injustice was out of question for a man of God like Guru Arjan, and the Guru suffered all such inhuman tortures with great courage and equanimity uttering the words "O God, Thy Will is sweet to me; Nanak craves nothing else but Remembrance of Thy Name".[2] The Guru passed on his divine spirit to the sixth Guru, Har Gobind, when for further torture his blistered body was being immersed in the cold water of nearby Ravi river. This unique martyrdom proved that even when it was known to Muslim Kazis who gave religious sanction to kill under the law of Yusa, that the Guru was a holy man, preacher of the same One God which was their God also, but for them not the Essence part but the other part of religion carried higher value.

Similarly Guru Tegh Bahadur, the ninth successor of Guru Nanak, had for twenty long years been worshipping God with love and devotion sitting in a cell at Bakala in Punjab, when the eighth Guru, Harkrishan declared him as his successor and passed on his own divine spirit to him before his death at Delhi in the year 1667 A.D. Guru Tegh Bahadur was subsequently executed in the year 1675 A.D. by the orders of

. Quoted in *Glimpses of Divine Masters*, p. 182.

2. Tera kiya meethha laage, Har naam padarath Nanak mange.
(Nanak V—Rag Asa).

Emperor Aurangzeb. This execution of a man of God was yet for another unique principle which the Sikh Gurus wanted to uphold and spread in the world. The principle was that every human being should have freedom of faith and worship. Coercion, force and tyranny in the matter of religious conversion was a crime, not credit. At that time by the orders of Aurangzeb conversion of Hindus to Islam was going on, on a mass scale in various parts of the country, specially in Kashmir. When a deputation of Hindus requested Guru Tegh Bahadur to save them from such forcible conversions, the Guru offered to sacrifice his life and he did so. The martyrdom of Guru Tegh Bahadur proved on the one hand that, the Muslim Kazis of Aurangzeb, who gave religious sanction (Fatwa) of death sentence to the Guru, treated faith in their Prophet as of higher value than faith in God which Guru Tegh Bahadur possessed so strongly. On the other hand it proved that the Sikh Gurus attached so much importance to the principle of 'Freedom of worship' for all human beings that they could sacrifice their lives for such a cause.

19

THE REAL PLACE OF RELIGION

The Objective of Khalsa Panth

The new religion, the Khalsa Panth was created by the great work and sacrifices of all the ten Gurus and for a great purpose. That purpose was to set right the previous ideas whereby religion was treated as one whole, each being claimed as superior to others, involving conversions and the accompanying coercions and tyrannies, breaking all norms of Dharma. The work before the Khalsa Panth, which was of utmost importance, was the propagation of Dharma. The world stood in dire need of such universal Dharma to which the Guru called as the highest amongst all that is treated as Dharma viz. "Remembrance of God's Name and performance of righteous deeds."[1] The Sikh Gurus included in Guru Granth Sahib all the norms of universal Dharma. From the fact that they also included therein the Spiritual Compositions of Hindu and Muslim saints of God, it is evident that their respective religions do have a part of such Dharma, to which those saints attached highest importance. Even when Hindu Shastras attach great importance to renunciate the active world, become Sanyasis and recluses to achieve Mukti, the Hindu Saints of God whose 'Bani' finds a place in Guru Granth Sahib, understood the principle of doing some vocational work, which principle is consistent with that stressed by the Gurus. Thus

1. Harko naam jap, nirmal karam. (Nanak V—Sukhmani).

Kabir was doing the work as a weaver of cloth, Nam Dev was a calico printer, Ravidas was doing the work of mending shoes as a cobler and so on. At the higher level of Dharma there is thus much scope of similarity and common ground but it is the lower Methodology part of religion which has all the differences.

With the broad-mindedness shown by the Sikh Gurus by inclusion in the scriptural book of the new religion the 'Bani' of Hindu and Muslim saints and with the most significant principle brought before the world by Guru Teg Bahadur by sacrificing his life for the freedom of faith and worship for all human beings, all are welcome to join the Khalsa Panth also by their own free will and choice, but religious conversion for increasing numbers was never the aim of this new religion. The real aim of the Panth was to infuse in all human beings the norms of Dharma as are contained in Guru Granth Sahib. For the Khalsa Panth therefore it is a good achievement if with its propagation of Dharma, the Hindus become good Hindus like Kabir, Nam Dev etc. and Muslims become good Muslims like Farid, Bhikhan etc.

However in order to be able to accomplish such a great job of spreading Dharma in the world, the Khalsa essentially has to be what Guru Gobind Singh intended him to be. He is to be a Saint of God and must have symbols of saintliness. He is to be a soldier to defend himself, his family, his people and his country and must have the symbols of strength. If Guru Gobind Singh had envisaged the Khalsa to possess so high a personality as to deserve his remarks 'Khalsa is my own special form', the Khalsa must not betray that confidence reposed in him by the Guru. In fact the Khalsa has the tradition of proving true to that confidence. Bhai Taru Singh, Bhai Mani Singh and numerous others, sacrificed their lives in the past and in the recent times, to prove true that confidence. That tradition must continue and symbols of five Ks prescribed by Guru Gobind Singh and other disciplinary rules must be treated as essential for the Khalsa.

Yet symbols are symbols and they represent something higher, mainly Saintliness and Strength as qualities of Dharma.

embodied in Guru Granth Sahib. Priority has to be attached to Dharma which is to be preached to mankind as a whole. Even between two essentials there can be a priority distinction. For instance air and water are both essential for human beings but priority is to be attached to air without which one cannot survive even for a short time. Accordingly if for the Khalsa the universal Dharma as highlighted in Guru Granth Sahib as well as the symbols of Khalsa Panth are both equally essential, priority must be attached to the former in the sense that it is universal Dharma which is not only to be practiced by the Khalsa, in order to become what his symbols signify, but also it is such Dharma which is to be preached and spread in the humanity at large.

When the Khalsa has to accomplish his main task of propagating Dharma, the foremost norm of which is stressed as worship of God in Guru Granth Sahib, it is also amply clarified therein what is the meaning of God-worship. It is not mechanical repitition of God's Name. Also God is not treated as a person sitting in some corner of Heaven. But as 'Nirankar' 'formless Spirit' He is present every where and in every human soul. Guru Nanak says "O Lord Thou art present everywhere, in regions of waters, earths, below, above, and in every human soul."[1] Every human being is house of God. Service of human beings is worship of God, and the Guru also says "If we serve others in this world; then only we can get a place of honour in the next."[2] Love and service of all human beings irrespective of their caste, religion, colour or nationality, is love service and worship of God. Guru Gobind Singh said to the Khalsa "Treat every human being as one and the same."[3] The Khalsa has the tradition of running free kitchens (Langars) in all main Gurdwaras where free food is served to all irrespective of their caste and creed so that no human being may suffer pangs of hunger or die in poverty for want of food. He has also the tradition to help the poor,

1. Jal thal mahiyal bharpur lina; Ghat ghat jot Tumari.
(Nanak I—Rag Bilawal).
2. Wich dunya sev kamaaiai; Tan dargeh baisan paaiyai.
(Nanak I—Sri Rag).
3. Manas ki jaat sabhai ekai pehchanbo. (Nanak X).

humble and innocent people and take their side if any tyrant causes suffering to them by acts of oppression, plunder, conversions by force and massacre. In fact the Khalsa always remembers the words of Guru Gobind Singh who said 'he has taken birth to spread Dharma, to save saintly people and uproot the evil doers.'[1] The humble innocent people come in the category of saintly people whom the Khalsa is duty-bound to protect against tyrants and evil doers.

Love and service of humanity necessitates possession of two other important qualities by the Khalsa and these are 'Toleration' and 'Forgiveness', The Sikh Guru themselves were full of these qualities and showed the same way to Khalsa. If before Guru Nanak, people who claimed to be 'religious' were so intolerant of faiths of others that they became bitter enemies calling each other infidels, the Sikh Gurus not only tolerated other religions but, as said earlier, they included the sayings of both Hindus and Muslim saints in Guru Granth Sahib along with their own. The Gurus were altogether free from narrow thinking, fanaticism and parochialism, which are traits capable of poisoning and suffocating human minds and intellects. Guru Nanak and his successor Gurus brought a soothing and pleasing breeze of broad-mindedness in the world. The sixth Guru, Har Gobind was imprisoned by the orders of Mughal Emperor Jehangir, who had also ordered torture to death his father, Guru Arjan Dev. But when subsequently he was released from Gwalior fort, at the intervention of Muslim saint, Mian Mir, who convinced the Emperor that the Guru was a Man of God, the Guru became friendly with Jehangir. This was so because Men of God do not carry rancour and spirit of revenge in their divine hearts which are rather full of love and spirit of forget, and forgive, remaining stead fast on their own job assigned to them by God. Similarly Guru Gobind Singh became friendly with Bahadur Shah, the son and successor of Aurangzeb who had ordered execution of his father, Guru Teg Bahadur and who was responsible for killing of his four sons. The Sikh Gurus had in abundance

1. "Dharam chalavan, San ubharan;
Dusht saban ko mool uparan."

the qualities of 'Toleration' and 'Forgiveness'. In fact, God Almighty is described in Guru Granth Sahib as full of mercy and forgiveness. He is watching human sins but goes on doing His own job of giving all the sustenance of their lives. Guru Gobind Singh says in praise of God "The protector of the humble, full of mercy and forgiveness, is watching human sins and shortcomings, but stops not giving essentials of their lives."[1] Thus if mercy and forgiveness are divine virtues and the Sikh Gurus were full of all such virtues, the Khalsa must also possess 'Toleration' and 'Forgiveness' in good measure to deserve his name of Khalsa.

But if on the other hand, instead of preaching all such qualities of Dharma to others, the Khalsa himself becomes intolerant of the faiths of others, surely he is going against the sublime principle of 'Freedom of Faith' preached by Guru Tegh Bahadur by sacrificing his life. The transgression of that high principle is still worse, if the Khalsa becomes intolerant of some sects which have some common and some different beliefs with his own beliefs, such as the sects of Namdharis, Udasis, Nirmalas or whatever other names they come to assume. Similarly if the Khalsa, instead of protecting the innocent people, resorts to use violence on them or kill them on some pretext, ignoring the principles of Toleration and Forgiveness, undoubtedly he is not on the path which was envisaged for the Khalsa by the Guru. In this vast world of diversity, praise and criticism have been going on side by side. Even the highest Teachers and Saints of God had both praise as well as criticism from the people. But they were broad minded enough neither to crave for any praise, nor to care for any criticism and went on performing their own job of doing good to all. For the Khalsa also the Guru wanted them to pray every day for the good of all (Sarbat ka Bhala) and also to put into practice this high principle.

It is quite evident that the Sikh Gurus intended that the new man of their vision, the Khalsa, should possess an ideal character. If he was given the outward appearance as of a

1. Din dayal Dia-nidh, dokhan dekhat hai par det na haare.
(Nanak X—Akal Ustat)

Saint, he was expected to have inner qualities also as of a Saint of God. However, human nature being what it is, all are not able to reach a high stage of perfection, all at once. If the Khalsa is treated as constituting the front line of the new Khalsa Panth, there is also a second line of the Panth. Those who believe in the ten Sikh Gurus and in Guru Granth Sahib embodying the spirit of ten Gurus, do not profess any other organised religion, but have not stepped up to reach the front line by adopting the symbols of five Ks., they constitute the second line of the Panth. They are generally called Sehjdharis but are an integral part of the Panth. This part deserves all love, honour and encouragement from the front line. On the other hand who after being in the front line, fall back to the second, they deserve discouragement.

However the most important question which demands serious consideration is how is it that the Khalsa has so far not been able to propagate in the world, to any appreciable extent, the qualities of Dharma as are highlighted in Guru Granth Sahib. Instead of goodness and qualities of Dharma why is sin and evil increasing in the world. Why has Khalsa not been able to make any dent so far in the prevalent situation and why, in fact, the Khalsa himself is lacking, to an appreciable extent the qualities of Dharma which were expected from him. There is a specific reason for this which, in main, is causing all such shortcomings. That reason is that so far even the organisation of the Panth is not complete. Guru Gobind Singh had himself recognised three parts of the Panth. While discontinuing the line of living Gurus, he transferred his own authority of leading the Khalsa in all matters, spiritual and secular to two authorities. Guru Granth Sahib was to be the evarlasting Guru of the Panth but Panj Piaras, subordinate to Guru Granth Sahib were to be leaders of the 'Sarbat Khalsa', the Khalsa as existing all over the world. The Panj Piaras constituted the second, and 'Sarbat Khalsa' the third part of the Panth. Guru Granth Sahib and the Sarbat Khalsa exist but the institution of Panj Piaras representing the Sarbat Khalsa, and possessing the high qualities as envisaged by the Guru, does not exist as a Central Institution. Guru Gobind Singh had set up this institution as he well visualised that when he will physically leave the scene of this world, this will be essential for the sake of the work for which the new Panth was created. After creating this institution on the Baisakhi day of 1699 A.D. he had therefore demonstrated that the Panj Piaras will be future living leaders of the Panth, by himself obeying their orders on several occasions. With such traditions set up by the Guru himself, it should not be difficult to find, out of the Sarbat Khalsa, five best Sikhs possessing the qualities expected from them. The infrastructure of such Central Authority in the form of the Centre of the Sikh world, Amritsar, the seat of weilding the Central Authority, the Akal Takht, are there but so far unfortunately the Panth has not given serious thought to install Shromani Panj Piaras at Akal Takht to complete its organisation.[1] However it can be hoped that at least before the year 1999 A. D. when the Khalsa Panth will be completing three hundred years of its existence, it will be able to complete its organisation. With the blessings of God Almighty, with inspiration from whom, Guru Nanak had originally planned the formation of the New Panth and Guru Gobind Singh had completed the structure thereof, the Khalsa Panth will then be on the high path to drive out evil suffering and darkness of falsehood and bring about light of Dharma, love and brotherhood in mankind. This constitutes the Real place of religion as also the objective of the Khalsa Panth.

1. *Note* : One scheme for constituting the Shromani Panj Piaras out of and representing the Sarbat Khalsa, was suggested by this author at the time of the Fourth Centenary Celebrations of the foundation of Amritsar City. That scheme received the blessings of late S. Hukam Singh President Kendri Sri Guru Singh Sabha, and many other scholars and well-wishers of the Panth. It was published by Kendri Singh Sabha in its pamphlet No. 3/77 and copies thereof are available from that Sabha and also from this author.

PART III

THE GREAT MARCH OF MAN TO TRUTH AND REALITY

20

THE GREAT MARCH OF MAN TO TRUTH AND REALITY

I—The Vedas and Shastras

That long time back man was like an animal walking on all fours, we do not have any definite knowledge, inspite of the surmises made by some western scientists. But we have more definite knowledge that ever since man stepped into era of civilisation, he has been on the march to find out Truth and Reality about the universe we live in. In such a search for Truth and Reality we have observed in the previous pages of this book and in its first volume the great contributions made by so many Avtars, Prophets, Gurus, Saints, Rishis, Sages and other great Souls. The greatest Truth which has been discovered by greatest number of those great Souls, is that there is One Supreme Lord of the whole universe. They also discovered the Reality about nature of that Supreme Lord. Two other vital Truths they discovered were about the nature of Man himself and what is objective of human life. Significant contributions regarding all these matters added by the Great Teachers of various World religions we discussed in Volume I. However Hindu religion is not only the most ancient but has so great a volume of religious literature covering so vast a ground that this comparative Study could not have been complete without undertaking a study of the various schools of philosophy of this great religion, as has been attempted in this present volume.

With the knowledge received through all such religious

philosophies, at this juncture it seems necessary to take a stock of the position where has mankind reached on this great march to Truth and Reality. Whatever we have come to know as Truth and Reality can any aspect thereof be treated as final or is there scope for further research, is the vital question before the world at present. A brief recapitulation of the whole position is therefore called for.

The Vedas are the earliest records available to the world showing the commencement of the research in the realm of Spirit and finding out Truth and Reality about that invisible realm. The Vedic sages settled in north western part of Bharat in the valley of beauty where flowed the mighty river Sindh with its five tributory rivers. The sages felt grateful to cosmic entities from which they were deriving benefits for their lives. Agni was giving them warmth and cooking their food, water coming from clouds was growing plants and trees for them, air was necessary for breathing and keeping them alive, the sun, moon and stars were giving them light and so on. As men of pure hearts the vedic sages felt so grateful to all such cosmic entities that they deified them and began to worship them. The Vedic Mantras are 'Samhitas' or Collections, predominantly in praise of all such cosmic entities but they do contain a hint about existence of One Supreme Power behind all. This concept of One God present in Samhitas, in a seed form, matured subsequently in the Upanisads which contained also a unique exposition about nature of God. The Vedic literature expanded further to its second and third parts of Brahamanas and Aranyakas, while its fourth part constituted by Upanisads, expanded so much that their number exceeded two hundred. All this literature was in the form of emotional thinking by Vedic Rishis, description of cosmic entities, praises of different deities and also of One Supreme deity, cravings from such deities of boons and necessities of life etc. However in the actual form as this literature existed and with its vast volume it could not exhibit clearcut principles of any system of philosophy. Hence from this literature six schools of Hindu Philosophy called six Shastras were constructed as have been explained earlier in some detail.

But before these Shastras matured as six schools of Hindu

Philosophy, three other indigenous philosophies intervened. These were Lokayata or Charvakya, Buddhism and Jainism. Lokayata was founded by Loukya Brahaspati who lived in the period of formation of Vedic Sanhitas and some Mantras are ascribed to him. For him there was no God, the world existed automatically, human Soul got destroyed with death of body and accordingly object of human life was eat drink and be merry. This philosophy had no place on the march to Truth and Reality, it was discarded by people of India, and it met its death long ago.

But its thread was taken up by Buddhism and Jainism. Buddhism also did not believe in any Supreme Power of God as also in permanency of human soul. However its founder, Gautam Buddha, was himself a noble soul who evolved an elaborate ethical code to be practiced by human beings. It is believed by many eminent scholars that Buddha remained silent about existence of God but did not positively refute His existence. He was sore about the Brahmanical ritualistic worship of cosmic entities and to stress the futility thereof he evolved the moral norms for practical human life. Buddha did not oppose Sansara or Transmigration of soul nor did he oppose the Law of Karma. He described Nirvana as the object of human life. But when human soul is not permanent according to Buddhism who suffers the rewards of Karma in Sansara and who enjoys the bliss of Nirvana, Buddhist Philosophy has never been able to advance any rational explanation. This philosophy also fell much behind on the March to Truth and Reality and was not tolerated, in the long run, by people of India to remain here to any appreciable extent even, though it spilled over to countries adjoining to India.

Jainism adopted a middle course. It said human soul is permanent but there is no Supreme Power of God. Like Buddhism it also believed in Law of Karma as well as in transmigration of Soul. But who controls the rewards of Karma in one life or spread over in many lives in the process of transmigration of soul, it has not been able to satisfactorily explain. For it the objective of human life is Sidhahood, which comes not by good actions but by nonaction, after exhausting all rewards both of good and bad actions. This philosophy has also not reached any stage in the march to Truth and Reality and failing to have an appeal to Indian people, it has remained almost at a stationery position all these about twenty-five centuries of its existence.

Out of the six Darsanas, the first four systems of Sankhya, Yoga, Vaisesika and Nayaya, as they were formulated by Kapila, Patanjli, Kanada and Gautama, did not have much concern with God. Out of these systems ideas about Yoga appear to have arisen in the minds of Indian sages earliest of all but it matured as a regular system later than Sankhya, whose finding regarding the Reality of our world were adopted by it. The Sankhya says there are two reals, the Pursha and Prakriti and both are self created. God is believed but as one of the Purusa whose function is to give the initial push to Purusa and Prakriti to join with each other so that human activity may get started. For Sankhya God is not the creator of the world nor is He a Supreme Power to whom Purusas should show any devotion. Prof. Hiriyanna therefore remarks "It (Sankhya) believes in the permanence and supremacy of spirit, but knows nothing of God...Devotion to God would consequently have no place in the discipline which is strictly in conformity with the Sankhya teaching."[1] The disciplines adopted by Sankhya are the eight fold disciplines of Yoga, while Yoga adopts the belief of Sankhya that God is not the Creator of Purusa and Prakriti. The main objective of Yoga was envisaged as achieving knowledge about human self and to develop both body and mind.

The Vaisesika-Nayaya the other pair of sister philosophies, substitute in place of Purusa and Prakriti of Sankhya, the Souls and Atoms, as the two Self-created realities. God gives these latter realities also the initial push to start functioning but is not their Creator. Subsequently all these four systems had to bring in God to occupy a more important and central place but keeping in view the high stage of Reality about God to which Vedanta reached, these four systems, in their classical form as envisaged by Kapila, Patanjali, Kanada and Gautama, did not reach even half way on that great march to Truth and

1. Hiriyanna, M., "The Sankhya", *Cultural Heritage of India*, Vol. III, 1953, p. 50.

Reality. For Sankhya and Yoga the responsibility for performing good or bad actions lies on Antahkarna or the 'internal organ' which is unconscious, being part of Prakriti and that unconscious part receives rewards of Karmas. The objective of human life is 'Kaivalya' which means complete separation of Purusa and Prakriti. In the state of Kaivalya the Purusa is conscious but without any feelings of pleasure or pain.

According to Vaisesika and Nayaya the Souls in their natural pure state do not have any consciousness. Consciousness is produced when the soul comes in contact with manas (mind) and other sense organs of the body. The objective of life is also Kaivalya or Mukti which is complete separation from body, mind and other sense organs and in this liberated state the soul does not have any consciousness and any feelings of pleasures and pains. It is not clear in this philosophy who is responsible for performing good and bad actions and receiving rewards thereof when Soul by itself does not possess any consciousness, knowledge and power of performing actions, while in the state of Kaivalya it lies as an unconscious stone.

The fifth Darsana, Purva Mimansa, does not concern itself with God and His nature. Vedas, according to it, have not been created by God but they are self-created. For Jaimini, the original author of Mimansa Sutras, as also for Sabra Swamin, Kumarila Bhatti and Prabhakara, who subsequently developed this system, the performance of physical actions such as offering sacrifices in Yajnas, burning of incenses in Homa and giving charities as Dana are of utmost importance to human beings and God has never been brought in at any stage in this system. Moral and spiritual values have also no place in it. Mahamahopadhyaya P. Tarkabhushan therefore says "The Mimansikas do not believe that knowledge divorced from ritualistic works can enable a man to rise to the full stature of his being."[1] The Mimansikas interpret the various Vedic Mantras as prescribing all the rituals they perform and they use those Mantras for chanting while performing the Yajna and Homa rituals. For them the Mantras are of all importance

1. Pramathanath, T., "Purva Mimansa", *Cultural Heritage of India*, Vol. III. 1953, p. 164.

for ritualistic purposes but Upanisads containing knowledge about existence and Nature of God do not carry any importance. Tarkabhushan therefore further remarks "Jaimini has not mentioned in his work anything about the existence of the Omniscient, Omnipotent and all merciful God, the Creator, Preserver and Destroyer of the universe. Sabra Swamin and Kumarila are also silent on that point."[1] Dr. Radhakrishnan also similarly says "It is unnecessary to say much about the unsatisfactory character of the Purva Mimansa as a system of philosophy. As a philosophical view of the universe it is strikingly incomplete. It did not concern itself with the problems of ultimate reality and its relation to the world of souls and matter. Its ethics was purely mechanical and its religion was unsound."[2] Hence it is evident that this system of Purva Mimansa stands at no stage in the March to Truth and Reality.

The Vedanta, the sixth Darsana, which is based on Upanisads, has divulged to the world the knowledge that God is One, the Only Reality, Omnipresent, Omniscient, Omnipotent, the Creator, Preserver and Destroyer of world and possessing all other excellent qualities. To such knowledge about God credence has been given by greatest number of Divine Souls, Saints, Prophets and Gurus who appeared in our world subsequent to the Upanisadic sages. Out of all the six Darsanas, the knowledge divulged by Vedanta not only reached the highest stage on the March to Truth and Reality, but it came at the earliest stage in the life of human civilisation as compared to other religious philosophies, also seeking Truth and Reality about our world. However a complication also arose when One God was described in Vedanta as having two aspects, the Brahman and Iswara.

In one aspect God could not be Creator, Preserver and Destroyer while in the other aspect He could be so. But if God is in reality One, He could not both be 'Creator' and 'not Creator'. But this splitting up into two, not only took place but further multiplied from two to many at the

1. *Ibid.*, p. 167.
2. Radhakrishnan, Dr. S., *Indian Philosophy*, Vol. II, pp. 428-29.

hands of different interpreters. According to interpretation of Ramanuja, as we observed, One Supreme God became many minor gods for practical purposes. Whereas for Sankra human Soul is not different from God-Soul, for Ramanuja Souls became different from God eternally. In fact Vedanta Sutras of Badarayana, on which depended both Sankra and Ramanuja, were themselves not clear on all these vital points and so were the Upanisads, whose number went on increasing indefinitely, even upto the time after advent of Islam as one Upanisad is called 'Alla Upanisad'. The later upanisads reflected different views, not reaching the heights of Truth and Reality as the earlier genuine Upanisads did. Dr. Radhakrishnan therefore says "The Sutra of Bedarayana reflects the indecision and vagueness characteristic of the Upanisads whose teachings it attempts to set forth and harbours within it many seeds of doubt and dissension."[1]

And he further says "They (Upanisads) began as a movement towards the liberation of the individual from the shackles of external authority and excessive conventionalism. They ended in rivetting the old chains. Instead of establishing new values for life they tended to propagate the tranditional ones."[2]

The knowledge about One Supreme God contained in the earlier genuine Upanisads is thus considered by numerous eminent scholars as higher and more sublime than that contained in the earlier three parts of Vedas which contain predominantly praises of cosmic entities, demands from them of various boons needed for life in this world, rituals and rites, as also magical charms, superstitious, prayers to harm others to gain something for self, etc., the latter being the matters appearing in Atharva Veda. The Vedanta based on the earlier genuine Upanisads, the works of Mahidasa, Aitereya, Raikava, Sandilya, Satyakama, Jabala, Jaivali, Udalaka, Svetaketu, Bhardvaja, Gargyayana, Pratardana, Balaki, Ajatasatru, Varuna, Yajnavalkya, Gargi and Maitreiye[3], therefore can be considered as reaching a very high stage on the great March of man to Truth and Reality.

1. Radhakrishnan, Dr. S., *Indian Philosophy*, Vol. II, p. 444.
2. *Ibid.*, Vol. I, p. 265.
3. *Ibid.*, p. 143.

21

THE GREAT MARCH OF MAN TO TRUTH AND REALITY

II—A New School of Hindu Philosophy

In the preceding chapter we discussed the position of the March to Truth and Reality according to the six recognised schools of Hindu Philosophy called the Six Darsanas or Shastras. However there is another new school of Hindu Philosophy which can not be ignored and demands to be explained in some detail. That is the school of Arya-Samaj Philosophy formulated recently in the nineteenth Century A.D. by Swami Daya Nand and explained in his book Satyarath Prakash. Like the Vedanta this new philosophy also says God is One, Omnipresent, Omniscient, Omnipotent and possessing other excellent qualities. But unlike Vedanta which says Iswara is the Creator of the entire universe, Arya Samaj says God is not the Creator of Souls as well as Matter. Swami Daya Nand says "The Soul was never created. It is beginningless like God and the material cause of the universe—primordial matter. The body and bodily organs were made by God, but they are all under the control of the Soul."[1] On being asked 'how many entities are eternal or beginningless, Swami Daya Nand replied "Three—God, the Soul and the Prakriti."[2] This

1. Daya Nand, Saraswati, Swami, *Satyarth Prakash*, tr. by Dr. Chiranjiva Bhardwaja, 1975, p. 221.
2. *Ibid.*, p. 243.

position is an advance over Sankhya philosophy, as it brings in God at the initial stage and says He is beginningless and eternal. But whereas for Vedanta God is the only Reality which is beginningless and eternal and the entire universe is the Creation of God (Iswara), this new Arya Samaj Philosophy reverts back to Sankhya in holding that Souls and Matter corresponding to the latters Purusa and Prakriti, are beginningless and eternal.

The Founder of Arya Samaj Philosophy has made a bold attempt to project that the various natural objects mentioned in the four Vedas for worship and adoration, such as Indra, Agni, Bhumi, Mitra, Varuna, Virat etc. are all names of One God representing His different qualities, and by his great scholarship in Sanskrit language, Swami Daya Nand has explained the roots from which these words can be taken as representing One God. His explanation of the root of Agni we have already indicated earlier in Chapter No. 3 on Vedas. A few other instances are quoted here for illustration:—

Indra means God because "Indra (from Idi-power) is one who is all-powerful."[1]

"Mitra (from nimid to love) means God because He loves all and is worthy of being loved by all."[2]

"Bhumi means God because "Bhumi is One who is abode of all and greater than all."[3]

Any attempt to project the existence of One Supreme God of all mankind takes the world higher in the march towards Truth and Reality. However about several natural objects which are stated by the Philosophy of Arya Samaj as indicating One God, mention exists in the four Vedas themselves describing them as Created objects. The Arya Samaj therefore holds that all such terms carry two meanings and it says:— "These names signify God in prayers, meditations, communions, or where such adjectives as Omniscient, Omnipresent,

1. *Ibid.*, p. 9.
2. *Ibid.*, p. 9.
3. *Ibid.*, p. 10.

Holy, Eternal and Creator of the universe qualify them. Whilst where the things under discussion are mentioned as created, protected or sustained, disintegerated or where such qualifying words as finite, visible are used they cannot be taken to signifying God, because He is neither subject to such changes as evolution or dissolution, nor is He finite or visible."[1] The Arya Samaj also strongly holds that the entire contents of the four Vedas Sanhitas are revelation from God Himself and therefore higher than the other parts of Vedas including the Upanisads which have lower value as commentaries explaining the Sanhitas. As to whom God revealed the Vedas the founder of Arya Samaj replied, "In the beginning God revealed the four Vedas, Rig, Yajar, Sama and Atharva to Agni, Vayu, Aditya, and Angira respectively"[2], as is mentioned in Satpatha Brahmana, and he further says "Among all men those four alone were purest in heart, therefore God revealed the true knowledge to them only" and "Brahma was instructed in the knowledge of the Veda through the medium of the four sages."[3]

Accordingly if the new Arya Samaj philosophy has personified as 'men', 'sages' the natural objects such as Agni, Vayu etc. and all such terms carry two meanings, the great praises and adoration of hundreds of natural objects contained in the four Vedas do apply both to One God and also to personified natural objects. Even though bringing in the concept of One God means rising higher on the march to Reality yet in this new philosophy not only the concept of two other beginningless and eternal entities of Souls and Matter, have also been brought in, parallel to God, but it has not been possible to eliminate the worship of 'Many', the natural objects, along with worship of one. If the Vedanta based on genuine Upanisads advanced much further from the stage of worship of 'Many' contained in four Veda Sanhitas and divulged a lofty concept of One Supreme God for human worship, the philosophy of Arya Samaj moved backward to the stage of

1. *Ibid.*, p. 6.
2. *Ibid.*, p. 236.
3. *Ibid.*, pp. 236-237.

Veda Sanhitas. It adopted that earlier way of adoration and worship of 'Natural Objects' contained in Sanhitas as of equal value with worship of One God, because it held the Veda Sanhitas, as a whole, the words of God and higher than Upanisads which, according to Arya Samaj, are words of human beings only. In fact the actual form in which the four Vedas exist, it is not easy to convert the praise and worship of 'Many' to worship of 'One, merely by interpretting the numerous terms by linking them with remotely relevant roots. This has been the findings of numerous eminent Hindu Sanskrit scholars who lived after Swami Daya Nand and whose views we have quoted earlier. All these Sanskrit Scholars could not give credence to the interpretation of Swami Daya Nand, contained in Satyarth Prakash for instance Dr. Suniti Kumar Chatterji, along with two other eminent scholars says "Though it is contended that the naturalistic interpretation of Vedic mythology sponsored by Yaska and followed by the early school of modern Vedists is not quite adequate, Vedic Nature—worship is undeniable."[1] Dr. S. Radhakrishnan similarly says "It is also recognised that the Vedic knowledge is much inferior to the true divine insight, and will not liberate us. Narda said 'I know the Rig Veda, Sir, the Yajur, the Sama Veda, with all these I know only the Mantras and the sacred books, I do not know the Self', The Mundka Upanisad says 'The two kinds of knowledge must be known, the higher and the lower. The lower knowledge is that which the Rig, Sama, Atharva Veda, Ceremonial, Grammer give...but the higher knowledge is that by which the indestructable Brahman is apprehended."[2] Dr. Radhakrishnan further says "The authority of the Vedas is to no small extent due to the inclusion of the Upanisads in them. It is often stated that Vedic knowledge by itself will not do. In the Chandogya Upanisad, Svetaketu admits that he has studied all the Vedas but is lacking in the knowledge, whereby what has not been heard of becomes heard of, what has not been thought becomes thought of, what has not been understood becomes understood. Narda tells Sanat

1. Chatterji, Dr. S. K., Pusalker, Dr. A. D., Dutt, Dr. N., "Editors' Preface", *Cultural Heritage of India,* Vol. I, 1958, p. 51.
2. Radhakrishnan, Dr. S., *Indian Philosophy*, Vol. I, p. 149.

Kumar that he has not the knowledge of the self, though he has covered the entire range of knowledge from the Vedas to snake charming—(VII-1-ff)."[1] Thus knowledge given to mankind by Upanisads is higher than that given by four Veda Sanhitas, as has been held by numerous Sanskrit Scholars, because the concept of One Supreme God matured in the Upanisads.

Further regarding the way of worship, the Founder of Arya Samaj stresses performance of two daily duties, 'Sandhyopasna' and 'Agnihotra' and he says about the latter "Devayagna, the second great Daily Duty, comprises Agnihotra the feeding of fire with clarified butter and aromatic substances for sanitary purposes—and associating with and serving devout and learned persons. These two duties—Sandhya and Agnihotra—are to be performed twice daily—morning and evening—it is only twice during 24 hours that day and night meet."[2] When asked how many 'ahuties' (spoonfuls) of clarified butter be used in fire each time of Agnihotra, he replied "sixteen 'ahutis' and a drachm and a half clarified butter in each ahuti at the least; but it is permissible to put more butter in each spoonful."[3] Thus thirty-two such spoonfuls of clarified butter are to be burnt in fire daily along with other aromatic substances in performing Agnihotra. This is however the 'Homa' ritual of Purva Mimansa and in this matter also whereas Vedanta, based on Upanisads stressed the worship of God by meditation on formless Brahman, the Arya Samaj is going back to the way of Purva Mimansa, treating the Veda Sanhitas and Brahmanas higher than the Upanisads.

Similarly giving all importance to four Sanhitas and Brahmanas, the Sudras are treated as not entitled to read Vedas neither entitled to Upanayana ceremony for wearing Yajnopavita and Swami Daya Nand says "An intelligent respectable Sudra, should also be taught all the Shastras,

1. Radhakrishnan, Dr. S., *Principal Upanisads*, p. 51.
2. Daya Nand, Swami, *Satyarth Prakash*, tr. by Dr. C. Bhardwaja, 1975, p. 37.
3. *Ibid.*, p. 39.

barring the Veda, but without performing his Upnayana."[1] About Manu Samriti, which provides very harsh discrimination against Sudras, Swami Daya Nand says "Among the Smrities the Manu Smriti alone is authentic."[2] From rational point of view Sudras also are human beings and they also require to read books of scripture, to worship God and achieve Mukti, as others do, but the snatching away of all privileges from them, to which, Arya Samaj gave all credence, means that God, who is also treated as Creator of Vedas, shows all favours to high caste but shows disfavour, and behaves as a veritable enemy of Sudras. With such treatment of Sudras God cannot be called just to all human beings and Arya Samaj is not depicting correctly the Reality of God. The Arya Samaj also holds that the Veda Sanhitas do not provide animal sacrifice in worship which was the way of worship adopted by Purva Mimansikas. Swami Daya Nand has held that Asvmedha Yajna does not mean horse sacrifice. In this matter also it could be highly praiseworthy, if by dint of scholarly interpretation, this cruel and primitive way of Hindu worship could be eliminated from the provisions of Vedas, but many Sanskrit scholars are unable to give credence to this claim of Arya Samaj also. For instance, Ganga Prasad, a former Chief Justice of a small state of India and an Ex-President of International Aryan League says, "The whole subject (of animal sacrifice) is highly controversial. The researches so far made by the Arya Samaj in this matter, though praiseworthy, are far from complete. Much has yet to be done before the Arya Samaj can satisfactorily place the subject of animal sacrifice in the Vedas, before the bar of public opinion."[3]

Further the Arya Samaj not only holds that human souls are self-created and are different from God, but it agrees with Ramanuja that they remain different from God in the state of Mukti. It holds that, after a time when a new Creation starts, from the state of emancipation or Mukti, the same souls

1. *Ibid.*, p. 40.
2. *Ibid.*, p. 142.
3. Devi Chand-Principal (D. A. V., College, Hoshiarpur) (tr. by), *Sama Veda*, p. 370.

come back to the world in the cycle of births and deaths. Swami Daya Nand advancing argument for this view says "In the place wherein emancipated souls live—otherwise called Heaven—there will be a great deal of hustling, crowding and jostling as there will be no end of increase in the population for the simple reason that immigration will be so great, whilst emigration will be nil."[1] And with nil emigration from Heaven to the world he says "If no souls come back from the state of emancipation the world should become bereft of them."[2] Regarding the belief of various Philosophies that God is Creator of universe including Souls, Swami Daya Nand says "If you say that God creates new souls, the material out of which He creates them will eventually run short; because a bank, however wealthy it may be that has a constant drain on it, but has no income, is sure to become bankrupt sooner or later."[3]

It is amply clear that Arya Samaj philosophy as explained in Satyarth Prakash differs substantially from Vedanta, not only in the matter of God's powers to create the world but also in the matter of nature of soul. Regarding the latter Swami Daya Nand says "Sankar is wrong in so far as he says that the Soul and the primordial matter as distinct from God do not exist and Ramanuja's belief that these three entities are eternally co-existent and yet the soul and God circumvented by Maya (Matter) are one is altogether absurd."[4]

Thus the Arya Samaj holds the Soul as separate from or 'Other' than God, and in this respect it resembles the Philosophy of Islam which also says the Soul as 'Other' than God. Islam treats it a sin of 'Shirk' to equate Soul with God. The Arya Samaj resembles Islam in another important aspect also. Islam treats Quran as the word of God dictated through Gabreil, an angel of God. Arya Samaj also treats the four Vedas as words of God dictated to four sages Agni, Vayu,

1. Daya Nand, Swami, *Satyarth Prakash*, tr. by Dr. C. Bhardwaja, 1975, p. 286.
2. *Ibid.*
3. *Ibid.*
4. *Ibid.*, p. 370.

Aditya and Angira, who in turn instructed Brahma in Vedic knowledge as we mentioned earlier. With Quran as the word of God, Islam has been treating itself superior to all other religions. Such superiority complex produced such a great zeal and religious fanticism that ever since its birth, Islam has been fighting religious wars with people of other religions, Christian, Jews, Hindus, Sikhs etc. and such enmities with others are going on even to this present time, in various parts of the world, as for instance Israil, Lebanon, Cyprus, Phillipines etc. The Arya Samaj Philosophy originated by Swami Daya Nand, of course with new interpretation of the contents of Vedic litrature, not only claimed Vedas as the words of God, but, as observed earlier, claimed Sanskrit as the language of God. In fact this two sided superiority, about the contents and language of Vedas has been the main basis of criticism of various other religions, Prophets and Saints of God, in the Satyarth Parkash. With the advent of Swami Daya Nand, consequently the earlier Islamic religious zeal and fanaticism was confronted with a stronger religious fanaticism of Arya Samaj, rising from the Bharat Desh itself. The clash of these two fanaticisms was evident in the beginning of the twentieth century, as the debate of superiority was reflected from Press and Platform in India. The unfortunate result was the Partition of this ancient land of sages and Saints of God, in the year 1947. What such superiority complexes have in store for this our Bharat Desh in future, only the time will tell.

It can, of course, be conceded that the Arya Samaj movement was intended to be a movement to reform the Hindu religion and extract it from the orthodoxy, in which it had been caught up at the time of advent of Swami Daya Nand. He rightly preached worship of One God discarding the worship of images and idols and in this matter the Arya Samaj has advanced higher than the rest of Hinduism, which continues to stick to image worship. Secondly it rightly tried to interpret Varna Dharma distinctions between Brahmans and lower castes, as not by birth but by 'Swabhava' or capability. But this caste system is so deeply rooted in Hinduism and Brahmans have so strongly entrenched themselves as superior to others that no reformer including the Founder of Arya Samaj has been able to make much dent in the fabric of the Caste system. On the other hand the Arya Samaj has added new dismensions to Superiority of Brahmans and of Hinduism in general as already mentioned above. From rational point of view a language is only a means to express in words the inner ideas of human beings. The superiority and merit attaches to the ideas and contents expressed through the language, not to the language itself. High Spiritual personalities with their hearts full of purity, sincerity, humility, love and longing for God, get inspiration from Him for their ideas and intuitions, which get recorded as their inspired words in the holy books of scripture. But if some one claims 'Only the contents and language of my holy book are God-created and Truest, such claims create self-pride and superiority complexes standing in the way of human equality and brotherhood. Whereas Self-pride blurrs one's vision to see things as they are, purity of heart and humility help to judge things rightly. If the Arya Samaj has, on the basis of its claim of Superiority criticised in Satyarath Prakash, Prophets of other religions and saints of God like Kabir and others, we quote the words of another Hindu eminent personality who was also a great Sanskrit scholar having an intense desire to reform Hinduism, but was free from Self-pride to see things as they were. He was Swami Dharma Theertha who says "Chaitanya roused a new enthusiasm in Bengal by the fervour of his devotion and self-surrender to the god of his heart, Sri Krishna and he too appealed for the recognition of human brotherhood. But Kabir, more than all others expressed the spirit of the age by boldly assailing idolatory, denying the divine authority of the Quran and the Hindu Vedas, and protesting against the neglect of the poeple's language and the exclusive use of Sanskrit. It was, however, reserved for Guru Nanak to become the founder of a new order of things a new nation free from many of the foibles and superstitions of the Hindus of those days. He taught that God should be worshipped as the One Supreme Invisible Being and that salvation lay in a life of virtue, purity and good works and implicit faith in and surrender to God".[1] Swami

1. Theertha, Swami Dharma, *The Menace of Hindu Imperialism*, 1946, p. 160.

Dharmaji conceded that Arya Samaj as a reformist movement intended to evolve a consolidated Hindu Nationalism but, as all those who judge things objectively do, he treats the criticism of other faiths, their Prophets and Saints of God, contained in Satyarth Prakash as unbecoming and he says "The Arya Samaj has continued to this day to be a champion of Hindu Nationalism, mixed however with an unbecoming animosity towards other faiths, which is not of course warranted by the broad principles of the Founder".[1]

It is most essential for a real reformer who wants to reform his people, to diagnose properly what is wrong with them, so that proper remedy could be applied. But if some one claims to be superior everything to which the word 'My' could be attached such as 'My religion' 'My holy book' 'My language' etc. to throw heaps of criticism on others, that is neither the right diagnoses of one's own side nor fair to others. Swami Dharma Theertha was more frank and truthful to say what he observed about his own side of Hinduism which he sincerely wanted to reform and apply the correct remedy. He therefore says "To complete the list of our perversions there is rising in the country a Hindu Nationalism, which is a traversity of all progress. This creed is being fostered by distinguished scholars and propagated both within and without the country with pride and religions fervour. It is marked by such claims as these; the Hindu civilisation is the best in the world. Hindu religion is the highest glory of man, Hindu institutions are the models of righteousness, Hindu Nationalism is peculiarly its own and unlike those of other Nations. The parading of these stupendous claims and exhibition of Self-esteem is only a prelude to a justification of all the evils and wickednesses of caste and priest crafts as the unique contributions of Hindu culture."[2]

In order to be treated as a real reformist movement of Hinduism, the Arya Samaj also needs to realise the evil of its deeprooted caste system and create equality amongst human beings. Also it shall have to bring about worship of One Supreme God by realising Him as Omnipotent and Omnipresent,

1. *Ibid.*, p. 262.
2. *Ibid.*, pp. 291-292.

Creator of the entire universe and present in all human beings. To sum up the views of this new school of Hindu Philosophy, as it is at present, the position is as follows :

Nature of God

God is One but He is not the Creator of Matter that exists in this vast universe ; Nor is He creator of Souls of living beings as both primordial matter and Souls are self-created. With such beliefs as indicated by the words in Satyarth Prakash 'If you say God creates new souls the material out of which He creates them will eventually run short' evidently enough God cannot be treated as All-powerful or Omnipotent in accordance with Arya Samaj Philosophy.

Nature of Man

All human beings cannot be treated as equal, having equal opportunities as Arya Samaj accepts the authority of Manu Smriti debarring Sudras to study Vedas and have other privileges which the higher castes have Human souls existed independently from God from the beginning and will continue to be so always.

State of Mukti

In the state of Mukti the soul will remain separate from God as was earlier held by Ramanuja. Regarding the way of worship to achieve Mukti this philosophy goes back to a certain extent, to the earlier way of Purva Mimansa.

With this overall position the only rational conclusion can be that this new school of Hindu Philosophy remains at a much lower stage of Truth and Reality than that to which Vedanta had reached on the basis of genuine Upanisads.

22

I—GURU NANAK'S SONG OF LOVE AND LONGING FOR GOD

We have already dealt with in some detail the Philosophy of Guru Nanak in the earlier chapters. Before we give a summary thereof, with due regard to the subject being dealt with in this Part, the Great March of man to Truth and Reality, we may see a few of the original words gushing out of the heart of Guru Nanak in love and longing for God.

> "O' My Lord God, I crave from thee one understanding, that I may never forget Thee, who are the One, the Giver while all living beings are receivers."[1]

"If there be a house studded all over by precious diamonds; And it may have a rub of nature's best perfumes : Yet O' my God, the longing of my heart is that all such wordly attractions may never divert my mind from love of Thy Name."[2]

"O dear, I cant live without Thee ; Bestow upon me the boon that I may always remain attached with Thy Name O'God; I have none else to whom I could cry out my mind and make a request. Thou art my Lord whom I serve and seek; Every breath of Nanak, Thy servant is for remembrance of Thy

1. Gura ik deh bujhaaiy; Sabna jia ka ik data so mai visar na jaaiy (Nanak I—Japji).
2. Moti ta mandar oosrai ratni ta hoe jarau;
Kastur kungu agar chandan leep aavai chao;
Mat dekh bhoola veesrai, tera chit na aavai naon (Nanak I—G.G.S., p. 14).

Name; Every bit of myself is a sacrifice unto Thee O' Lord."[1]

"I seek the dust of Thy lotus feet O' God; Day and night I cry like a Papiha (Indian cuckoo) in thirst for a drop of rain; Bestow on me the grace of Thy Name; which is the only water that can quench. Nanak's thirst"[2],

"O' God, Thou art Supreme Lord, Thy greatness is beyond my power to describe fully ; I describe only to the extent Thou giveth me the power; I possess not any sense independently from Thee; Grant me understanding O' God, that I may go on singing Thy praises; And remain absorbed in the Truth of Thy Will."[3]

The response of God to a man who sincerely seeks His love is depicted thus by Guru Nanak :—"If thou seek to play the game of My love; Place thy head on thy palm and proceed forward towards Me; (completely shun the pride of thyself, the Haumai); If thou are treading the path of My love; Then there should be no hesitation to offer the sacrifice of thy head."[4]

1. Tudh bahj piare kev raha;
Sa vadiaiy deh jit naam tere laag raha;
Dooja nahi koe jis aage piare jaae kahan;
Sevi Sahib aapna avar na jacho koe;
Nanak ta ka das hai bind bind chukh chukh hoe;
Sahib tere naam vitu bind bind chukh chukh hoe;
(Nanak I—G. G. S., p. 660).
2. Har charan kamal makrand lobat, mano andino mohe aahi piaasa. kirpa jal deh Nanak sarang ko hoe jate tere naam vaasa, (Nanak I—G.G. S., p. 663).
3. Tu sultan kaha hau mian teri kavan wadaiy;
Jo tu deh so haha suami, mai moorakh kehn na jaaiy;
Tere gun gava deh bujhaiy, Jaise sach mai raho rajaaiy.
(Nanak I—G.G.S., p. 795).
4. Jo tau prem khelan ka chao; Sir dhar tali gali meri aao; It marag pair dhrijai, sir deejai kaan no keejai (Nanak I—G. G. S., p. 1412).

II—THE PHILOSOPHY OF GURU NANAK A SUMMARY

Nature of God

God is One without a second like Him. He is an all-pervading incorporeal spiritual Power. He is Creator of the entire universe that we see or do not see, we can imagine or can not imagine. He is all-Powerful and all powers emanate from Him. No power whether of Creation, Sustenance or Destruction, exists independent of Him. He Himself is Self-created and none else. Souls of jivas and Matter are His creation. He has entered His own creation and is immanent therein. He has a Sovereign Will of His own and all the activity that has been going on in this universe, is going on and will go on in future, is within His overall Will. But His nature is all-truth, all-consciousness and all-bliss (Sat-Chit-Anand). He is thus the direct source of truth, virtue, goodness and happiness but is not direct source of untruth, evil, sorrow and pain. He is perfectly just to all souls whom He sends to life in the world. He gives initially equal opportunities to all without showing favour or disfavour to any. He is all love and mercy which He showers on those who seek His love and mercy with sincere hearts.

Nature of Man

Even when all the activity which is going on in the universe is within the overall Sovereign Will of God, in the matter of actually creating all such activity God has established a 'Rah' or 'Method' or 'Law.'[1] Under the Law while creating human

1. Hukmi Hukam chalaae 'Rah'
Nanak vigsai veparvah
(Nanak I—Japji).

beings He has added with every Soul a temporary covering of consciousness which calls itself 'I'. This 'I' which is termed 'Haumai' in the Philosophy of Guru Nanak, has been given the power of thinking, volition and exercising choice to perform, with the aid of organs of the body, actions both good and evil. Such a choice of actions has come to be called Law of Karmas (actions). All human beings with their I-consciousnesses originally getting equal opportunities perform good or bad actions in the course of their lives in one or more bodies and earn merits or demerits, which create differences in them. These I-consciousnesses on account of their merits or demerits, become subject to pleasures and pains of life and also move in the circle of births and deaths as a consequence of the Law of actions. The inner core of human Soul is not different from the all-pervading, Eternal God but it is not correct to say 'I am God' as 'I' represents the God-created temporary consciousness which is subject to births and deaths as well as pains and sorrows, while God is not subject to these. In this matter this Philosophy of Guru Nanak, therefore differs from Vedanta which says 'I am Brahman', 'This Self is Brahman' etc.

This Philosophy of Guru Nanak also differs from that of Islam which holds human soul (abd) as 'Other' than God remaining always 'Other' when the soul is said to enjoy, after death, the pleasures of Bahisht (Heaven) or pains of Dozakh (Hell).

When the I-consciousness or Haumai, with its will bestowed upon it by God, performs good actions, this human will becomes consistent with the higher God-Will, which is the source of all-goodness, virtue and bliss, and in this case it can be said that the higher God-Will has prevailed while the lower human will or Haumai is not asserted.[1] But all evil actions being inconsistent and against the Will of God, the Haumai performing such actions becomes the real source of all evils and pains prevailing in the world. According to Guru Nanak's

1. Nanak Hukmai je bujhai ta Haumai kahe na koe—(If one realises and acts according to the Will of God, then none says Haumai is asserted) (Nanak I—Japji).

philosophy, therefore, no outside power, no angel revolting against Will of God, no Satan and no worldly wealth (Maya) is source of evil and pain but it is Haumai which is inside human beings that causes all evil and pain. This Haumai takes the form of pride of self and selfishness present in a large measure in our world. It is the Haumai that is forming a shadow and a curtain, prevents the Soul to shine forth as Pure God spirit from the inner self of human beings. It is this situation that enables to understand clearly what is the objective of human life.

The Object of Human life

The object of human life is Mukti or Liberation of human Soul, as in the case of so many other religious philosophies we have already discussed. But in this case of the Philosophy of Guru Nanak, the Soul which gives life to human body, is part of the unlimited ocean of life, the all-pervading God-consciousness. Mukti comes when the God-created temporary I-consciousness or Haumai separates from the Soul. Haumai is the source of all evil and pain while God is the source of all goodness and happiness. When Haumai drops down the Soul rejoins the all-pervading God-Consciousness and thus Mukti is a state of bliss and happiness. The state of Mukti according to the philosophy of Guru Nanak is therefore different from Kaivalya of Sankhya and Yoga where the conscious Purusa remains not only without pain but without bliss or happiness also. It is also different from Kaivalya of Vaisesika and Nayaya where the soul remains at rest but even without any consciousness. This philosophy resembles Vedanta in one aspect but differs in others. It agrees with Vedanta that human Soul is not different from the all-pervading and eternal God-Consciousness in so far as its inner core part is concerned. But whereas Vedanta holds such God-Consciousness as the Only Reality all else being unreal, Guru Nanak's philosophy has divulged that the God-created I-Consciousness (Haumai), attached to every soul is not eternal yet real. Vedanta says Mukti means dropping down of Ignorance or Avidya when Vidya, knowledge or 'Gyan' of that Single Reality of God-Consciousness shines forth in a jiva. But if jivatman or human soul is not different from God, and God is all-knowing, with whom exists Ignorance or Avidya and from whom it drops down is not satisfactorily explained by Vedanta nor it clarifies who falls in transmigratory circle of births and deaths and suffers pains and sorrows.

The existence of a separate temporary I-consciousness or Haumai along with human soul, as divulged in the Philosophy of Guru Nanak, is within the experience of every human being and no one can deny this perceptible reality. In this philosophy greatest stress has been laid on Remembrance of God's Name which brings in human minds the light of God-consciousness, reducing and replacing gradually the I-consciousness, the Haumai. At an advanced stage of this process the Haumai is nearly eliminated and a human being experiences the real happiness of which God is the source. This brings in the state of Jiwan-Mukti, which extends further to complete Mukti at death of body. That means rejoining God-Consiousness the unlimited ocean of bliss and happiness. To this extent the state of Mukti can be judged as all-bliss, by human experience in the state of Jiwan-Mukti. But in the Philosophy of Guru Nanak, it is also greatly stressed that God is 'Beant' meaning that His ways are beyond the reach of human understanding to be known fully even upto the remote future. It can not therefore be said that after Mukti the souls will always remain separate from God even upto and beyond Parlaya and coming of a new Creation. This Philosophy of Guru Nanak therefore differs also from Vedanta as interpretted by Ramanuja, who held that the Souls always remain separate in the state of Mukti. This, as mentioned earlier, had attracted the ridicule from eminent philosophers that Ramanuja had come back to tell this tale after once achieving Mukti. As the latest school of Hindu philosophy, that of Arya Samaj, also describes the state of Mukti as Ramanuja does, where the Souls always remain separate from God, the philosophy of Guru Nanak differs from this latest Hindu philosophy in this matter also.

A vital question which needs to be answered and included in this Summary, is in what way the Haumai can be dropped down from the Soul to achieve Mukti according to Philosophy of Guru Nanak. The answer, in brief, is that Haumai can be dropped down and Mukti is achieved by Simrin' or Meditation and 'Seva' or Service. But Simran should be on Real God. An image or idol of a god or goddess can be of a personality and a personality has to be either male or female and also subject to birth and death and having other limitations. The Real God is not subject to any limitations whatsoever and is the Eternal, all-pervading, formless spiritual Power which is present every where and in every living being. Meditation should be on such complete and Real God which can only be represented by God's Name. The Guru has therefore said "Meditation is to be on the Complete God who is represented by His Name; Nanak has realised that Complete Real God; All should sing His praises."[1] For singing His praises and meditation on His Name, one who sings and meditates, has to be separate from or second to God as part of His Creation, which is mentioned as 'Dooiy Qudrat saajiai' or second to His Self. The Guru therefore says "From One Supreme God the creation has come into existence as Second to Him; But Creator is One whose Will prevails supreme; Jivatman, the created second, when realises the One Supreme; Through the way of meditation as divulged by Guru's words, he reaches the door of God; Acting on True Guru's guidance one ultimately rejoins God; When he eliminates the inner duality or Haumai."[2] Meditation on God's Name and singing His praises produces in human minds such an understanding that he begins to say O' God Thou art the Creator, Thou art the Sustainer, Thou art bestower of all bounties of life, Thou art everything, etc. and correspondingly the ideas of I-ness, Self-pride and Selfishness get subdued and ultimately Haumai gets eliminated paving the way to Mukti. This method of subduing and eliminating Haumai by saying words such as 'O God Thou

1. Poora Prabhu aradhia, poora ja ka naaon;
Nanak poora paaia, poore ka gun gaao.
(Nanak V—Sukhmani).
2. Ekas te sab dooja hua; Eko vartai avar na bia;
Dooje te je Eko jaanai;
Gur kai sabad, Har dar nisanai;
Satgur Bhete ta Eko paae;
Vicho dooja thhak rahaae. (Nanak III—G.G.S., p. 842).

art everything' is amply demonstrated by the Gurus in their 'Bani' recorded in the holy volume of Guru Granth Sahib. The Gurus also say in great humility such words as 'I am nothing' 'I am a sinner' 'I have no sense' etc. because they speak as if standing before God and on behalf of all human beings whom they want to show the way to eliminate Haumai and rejoin God. But the words 'Thou art every thing' do not signify that God is also the source of evil, neither do the words 'I am nothing' on behalf of human beings signify that human I-ness does not possess the will to do good or bad actions. God is not the source of evil and as some other philosophies believe, it is not He who misguides some human beings towards evil. God's fundamental quality as declared by Guru Nanak is He is 'Nirvair' or absolutely just. He does not arbitrarily push someone to do evil acts and suffer the pains thereof, and push others towards goodness and enjoy the happy consequences thereof.

The second main virtuous action for achieving Mukti is 'Seva'. As stressed emphatically by Guru Nanak 'Seva' should be of humanity at large as God resides in every human heart. The Guru says addressing his own eyes but implying guidance to all human beings "The whole world that you see is the picture of God and you are seeing God Himself; By the grace of Guru the realisation has come that God is residing in every human being that the eyes are seeing; None is without Him; Says Nanak before meeting a True Guru the eyes were blind, but after meeting him, they have received the clear vision to realise Him in all human beings."[1] Accordingly service of human beings, who are in need, who are in trouble, is service of God. God loves those who love human beings and relieve their sufferings by serving them. Some human beings may be in trouble and suffering due to oppression by others as the forces of goodness of God and evil of Haumai are existing

1. Ih vis sansar tum dekhde,
Ih Har ka roop hai Har roop Nadri aaia,
Gurparsadi bujhia ja vekha Har ik hai,
Har bin avar na koiy, kahai Nanak ih netar andh se,
Satgur miliai dib drisht hoiy—(Nanak III, G.G. S., p. 922).

side by side in our world and the latter cause trouble and suffering. The Philosophy of Guru Nanak has envisaged a new ideal man, the Khalsa, possessing qualities both of Saintliness and Strength. Sometimes the Khalsa can be called upon to serve others by saving them from oppression and tyranny of evil doers. In such a situation he is to function not merely as a soldier but both as a Saint and a soldier. He is to use strength by sword or other weapon only for righteous and defensive purposes, but never for unrighteous and offensive purposes and never against any innocent human being. Guru Gobind Singh had said "When all other means have been exhausted it is within righteousness to lift in hand the sword."[1] It is quite clear that strength is to be used by lifting the sword and using other weapons, only after exhausting all other means of correcting the evildoer tyrant, but never before exhausting such other means. The Khalsa himself is never to become an oppressor and tyrant because while using strength he has to continue to behave as a Saint also. To check the evildoers and to put a stop to the forces, which are advancing in our world, the foremost means which is of highest importance is what Guru Gobind Singh had declared 'Dharam chalavan' or propagating Dharma. Before lifting the sword the Khalsa is therefore, called upon to do that foremost job of spreading the light of Dharma as is contained in Guru Granth Sahib and that will remove the darkness of evil and this will also be the highest 'Seva' of humanity.

The world can certainly be benefitted if this Philosophy of Guru Nanak is propagated with all sincerity and determination. It has been built up by unique efforts made by the ten Gurus and by making unique sacrifices. However it appears to be a fact, that the world at large is generally unaware about it and the blame certainly lies on the Sikhs themselves who have not been able to make so far adequate efforts to do this job. A theory is best propagated by making a practical demonstration thereof. The Khalsa is therefore called upon to understand himself the high Philosophy of

1. Chukar az hama heelte dargushat;
Halal ast burdane ba shamsheer dast. (Nanak X—Zafarnama).

Guru Nanak and to put it into practice by living according to it and then to propagate it to the world.

It is this Philosophy of Guru Nanak which gives highest place to the worship of One God, who is common to all religions and thus can unite the humanity. It is this philosophy which gives no place to Self-superiority, Self-pride and Selfishness, the factors which divide humanity. It is this philosophy which envisages a 'Man of God' (Wahiguru ji ka Khalsa) to spread the universal Dharma to all mankind. It is this Philosophy of Guru Nanak which envisages the 'Victory of God' (Wahiguru ji ki Fateh) so that the virtuous qualities of God like Truth, Justice and Mercy may be victorious and prevail in the world, no one may oppress and tyranise over others and all may live in peace and affection. It is this philosophy that envisages this world to become as a kingdom of merciful God Himself where love and humility may prevail. Such a unique picture of the world is, in fact, painted in the holy Guru Granth Sahib so that the Khalsa Panth may always keep in view such an objective for which this new Panth has been created, the Guru says

> "Now the Will of merciful God is ruling human minds None is subjected to tyranny and coercion. As love and humility now prevail; And kingdom of God has come on earth".[1]

Wahiguru ji ka Khalsa; Wahiguru ji ki Fateh.

1. Hun hukam hoa Mehrvan da;
Pai koe na kisai rijhanda;
Sab sukhali vuthhia;
Ih hoa halemi raj jio.
(Nanak V—Sri Rag, G.G.S., p. 74).

SELECT BIBLIOGRAPHY

Bhattacharya, Darsanasagra, H., "The Philosophies", *The Cultural Heritage of India, Volume III.*

Bhave, Vinobha, *Talks on Geeta.*

Chatterji, Dr. S.K., Dutt, Dr. N., Pusalker Dr. A.D. Bose, N.K., "The Early Phases", *The Cultural Heritage of India, Vol I.*

Chinmayananda, S., *The Holy Geeta.*

Chowdhuri, N.C., *Hinduism, A Religion to Live By.*

Das Gupta, Dr. S.N., *History of Indian Philosophy.*

Dawood, N.J. (tr. by), *The Koran.*

Dayanand, Swami (tr. by. Bhardwaja Dr. C), *Satyarth Prakash.*

De, Dr. S.K., Ghoshal Dr. U.N., Pusalker, Dr. A.D. Hazra, Dr. R.C. "Ithasas, Puranas, Dharma and Other Sastras", *The Cultural Heritage of India, Vol. II.*

Devichand, (tr. by.), *The Sama Veda.*

Gambhirananda, S. (tr. by), *Brahma Sutra Bhashya of Sankaracharya.*

Gambhirananda, S. (tr. by), *Eight Upanisads.*

Ghosh, Aurobindo, *On Yoga, The Synthesis of Yoga.*

Ghosh, Aurobindo, *The Foundation of Indian Culture.*

Griffith, R.T.H., (tr. by), *Hymns of Rig Veda.*

Gupta, Dr. H.R., *History of the Sikhs.*

Jagjit Singh, S., *The Sikh Revolution.*

Jodh Singh, Bhai, *Gurmat Nirnai.*

Karam, J.J., *Guru Nanak, Paper in International Seminar, 1969.*

Kartar Singh, Dr., *Fundamentals of Sikhism.*

Macauliffe, M.A., *The Sikh Religion.*

Max Muller, (tr. by), *The Upanisads.*

Mitra, Dr. P., *Life and Society in the Vedic Age.*

Muhammad Ahmad, Pir S., *Hazrat Sarmad Shahid.*

Pandit; M.P., *Highways of God.*

Purani, A.B., *Studies in Vedic Interpretation.*

Radhakrishnan, Dr. S., *The Principle Upanisads.*

Radhakrishnan, Dr. S., *Indian Philosophy*, *Vol. I and Vol. II.*

Ramna, Maharishi, *Talks with Sri, 1972.*

Ranbir Singh, *Glimpse of Divine Masters.*

Sale, G., (tr. by), *The Koran.*

Stamp, A.H., *Other Nations Colonies.*

Theertha, Swami D., *The Menace of Hindu Imperialism, 1946.*

Thibaut, G. (tr. by), *Vedanta Sutras with Sankara Bhashya.*

Tillich, P,, *What is Religion.*

Vivekananda, Swami, *Karma Yoga.*

Vivekananda, Swami, *Practical Vedanta.*

Wazir Singh, Dr., *Humanism of Guru Nanak, A Philosophic Enquiry.*

Whitney. W.D. (tr. by), *Athrva Veda Samhita.*

Wilson, W.H. (tr. by), *Rig Veda Samhita.*

Yusuf Ali, A. (tr. by), *Illustrious Koran.*